Program Guide

GRADES 1–2

Copyright © by Houghton Mifflin Harcourt Publishing Company

All rights reserved. No part of this work may be reproduced or transmitted in any form or by any means, electronic or mechanical, including photocopying or recording, or by any information storage or retrieval system, without the prior written permission of the copyright owner unless such copying is expressly permitted by federal copyright law. Requests for permission to make copies of any part of the work should be submitted through our Permissions website at https://customercare.hmhco.com/contactus/Permissions.html or mailed to Houghton Mifflin Harcourt Publishing Company, Attn: Compliance, Contracts, and Licensing, 9400 Southpark Center Loop, Orlando, Florida 32819-8647.

Printed in the U.S.A.

ISBN 978-0-358-46204-0

4 5 6 7 8 9 10   0607   30 29 28 27 26 25 24 23 22

4500845202

r1.21

If you have received these materials as examination copies free of charge, Houghton Mifflin Harcourt Publishing Company retains title to the materials, and they may not be resold. Resale of examination copies is strictly prohibited.

Possession of this publication in print format does not entitle users to convert this publication, or any portion of it, into electronic format.

Contents

Authors and Advisors 4
Connected Teaching for Today's Educators 6

INTRODUCTION
Build, Connect, and Grow. 7

PROGRAM TOUR 19
Connected Teaching 20
Student and Teacher Resources 22
Year at a Glance................................ 24
Module at a Glance............................. 26
Week at a Glance 28
Connected Teaching with Ed: Your Friend in Learning® .. 32
Grow Your Craft with HMH Literacy Solutions™ 34

TEACHING AND LEARNING 37

PLANNING AND PACING
Planning Made Easy............................ 38
Scheduling and Remote Teaching Support 40
Implement Effective Classroom Routines 42

BUILD KNOWLEDGE AND LANGUAGE
Knowledge Networks 44

FOUNDATIONAL SKILLS
Phonological Awareness 46
Phonics and Fluency 48
Spelling and Handwriting 50
High-Frequency Words......................... 52

ORAL LANGUAGE AND VOCABULARY
Academic Vocabulary 54
Generative Vocabulary and Vocabulary Strategies 56
Speaking and Listening......................... 58

READING
Text Sets and Text Complexity 60
Comprehension Skills and Strategies 62
Dialogic Reading with Read Alouds............... 64
Shared Reading............................... 66
Writing in Response to Texts 68
Independent Reading 70

OPTIONS FOR DIFFERENTIATION
Small-Group Instruction........................ 72

WRITING WORKSHOP
Writing Process............................... 74
Grammar...................................... 76

RESEARCH
Inquiry and Research........................... 78

Research Foundations.......................... 80

PROGRAM GUIDE

ASSESSMENT AND DIFFERENTIATION 83
- Data and Reporting 84
- Assessments at a Glance. 86
- Growth Measure 90
- Screening, Diagnostic, and Progress-Monitoring Assessments 92
- Formative Assessments 94
- Assess Writing and Projects............................ 96
- Document Students' Growth........................... 98
- Provide Differentiated Support and Intervention 100
- Support English Learners............................... 102
- Meet the Needs of Accelerated Learners 104
- Meet the Needs of Special Populations........... 106
- Use Digital Features for Accessibility 108

CLASSROOM COMMUNITY 111
- Make the Best Use of Your Classroom 112
- Get Started with Literacy Centers 114
- Embed Social and Emotional Learning 118
- Create a Culturally Responsive Environment 120
- Communicate with Families 122

¡ARRIBA LA LECTURA!............................ 125
- Welcome to *HMH ¡Arriba la Lectura!* 126
- Hispanic and Universal Literature 128
- Dual Language Program Planning 134

LITERATURE RESOURCES 143
- Module Topics and Text Sets 144
- Text Complexity 152
- Notice & Note 156
- Rigby® Leveled Library.................................. 160

- Credits... 167

Contents 3

Authors and Advisors

Alma Flor Ada, Ph.D.
Professor Emerita, University of San Francisco; internationally renowned expert in bilingual literature and literacy; author of over 200 award-winning books, both academic and for young readers; a leading mentor in transformative education

Kylene Beers, Ed.D.
Nationally known lecturer and author on reading and literacy; national and international consultant dedicated to improving literacy, particularly for striving readers; coauthor of *Disruptive Thinking*, *Notice & Note: Strategies for Close Reading*, and *Reading Nonfiction: Notice & Note Stances, Signposts, and Strategies*

F. Isabel Campoy
Award-winning bilingual author of over 150 children's books of poetry, theater, stories, biographies, art, and culture; internationally recognized scholar, educator, and translator; a member of the North American Academy of Spanish Language

Joyce Armstrong Carroll, Ed.D., H.L.D.
Nationally known consultant on the teaching of writing, with classroom experience in every grade from primary through graduate school; codirector of Abydos Literacy Learning, which trains teachers in writing instruction; coauthor of *Acts of Teaching: How to Teach Writing*

Nathan Clemens, Ph.D.
Associate Professor, University of Texas, Austin; researcher and educator with a focus on improving instruction, assessment, and intervention for students with reading difficulties in kindergarten through adolescence

Anne Cunningham, Ph.D.
Professor, University of California, Berkeley; nationally recognized researcher on literacy and development across the life span; coauthor of *Book Smart: How to Develop and Support Successful, Motivated Readers*

Martha C. Hougen, Ph.D.
Teacher educator focused on reforming educator preparation to better address the diverse needs of students; coeditor and contributing author of *Fundamentals of Literacy Instruction & Assessment Pre-K–6*

Dr. Tyrone C. Howard, Ph.D.
Professor of Education at the Graduate School of Education and Information Studies and Associate Dean for Equity, Diversity, and Inclusion at the University of California, Los Angeles; Director, UCLA Pritzker Center for Strengthening Children and Families; author of several published articles and books, including *Expanding College Access for Urban Youth*

Elena Izquierdo, Ph.D.
Associate Professor of teacher education at the University of Texas, El Paso; researcher and practitioner with a focus on dual-language education, biliteracy, and educational equity for English learners

Carol Jago, M.A.
Nationally known author and lecturer on reading and writing with 32 years of classroom experience; author of *With Rigor for All* and the forthcoming *The Book in Question: How and Why Reading Is in Crisis*; national consultant who focuses on text complexity, genre instruction, and the use of appropriate literature in the K–12 classroom

Erik Palmer, M.A.
Veteran teacher and consultant whose work focuses on how to teach oral communication and good thinking (argument, persuasion, and reasoning), and how to use technology in the classroom to improve instruction; author of *Well Spoken* and *Good Thinking*

Robert E. Probst, Ph.D.
Professor Emeritus, Georgia State University; nationally known literacy consultant to national and international schools; author of *Response & Analysis* and coauthor of *Disruptive Thinking*, *Notice & Note: Strategies for Close Reading*, and *Reading Nonfiction: Notice & Note Stances, Signposts, and Strategies*

Shane Templeton, Ph.D.
Foundation Professor Emeritus of Literacy Studies at the University of Nevada, Reno; researcher and practitioner with a focus on developmental word knowledge; coauthor of *Words Their Way*

Julie Washington, Ph.D.
Professor, Georgia State University; researcher with an emphasis on the intersection of cultural dialect use, literacy attainment, and academic performance; author of numerous articles on language and reading development, and on language disorders in urban children growing up in poverty; consultant for *iRead*, *System 44*, and *READ 180* Universal

Contributing Consultants

David Dockterman, Ed.D.
Lecturer at Harvard University Graduate School of Education whose work focuses on turning research into effective, innovative practice to meet the variable needs of all learners; advisor on *MATH 180* and *READ 180* Universal

Jill Eggleton, QSO (Queen's Service Order in Literacy and Education), Ed.D.
International consultant and teacher with over 35 years of teaching and administration experience; trains and inspires educators in how to incorporate balanced-literacy methods in the classroom; Adjunct Professor, Sioux Falls University; Margaret Mahy Literacy Medal award winner; author of over 1,000 children's books, poetry, and teacher resources

Connected Teaching for Today's Educators

Dear Educators,

At HMH, **we have been listening** to your needs. Lean on us to help you

- connect students to the right **instruction**
- deliver flexible and innovative learning experiences built on the foundations of **best teaching practices** and **educational research**
- **bridge the digital divide** with instruction available in both print and digital formats, accessible online and offline
- provide a **reliable and valid growth measure** that monitors progress and achievement
- implement traditional classroom teaching and the tools to deliver instruction through **remote learning**
- foster students' **social and emotional growth** and build resilience through embedded SEL support
- teach with continuous, connected **professional learning** . . . and **do what you do best**

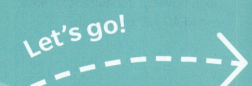

Take a look!

This Program Guide is **your professional companion** to help you to learn about your new program and to **build, connect,** and **grow** with *HMH Into Reading* and *HMH ¡Arriba la Lectura!*

Introduction

Introduction

BUILD

- A Love of Reading
- Foundational Skills
- Topic Knowledge & Vocabulary
- Reading Comprehension

CONNECT

- Literacy Instruction & Content Areas
- Student Choice & Independent Practice
- Effective Writing & Communication
- Assessment Data & Differentiated Support for All Learners

GROW

- Social & Emotional Learning
- Continuous, Connected Learning

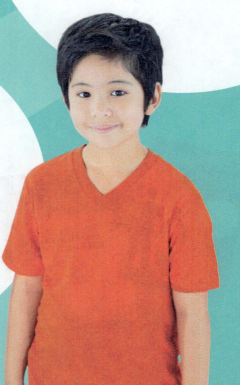

BUILD...

A Love of Reading

Get *Into Reading* with a wealth of award-winning, **culturally relevant** texts in a wide variety of **genres**.

Inspire readers with engaging texts and ignite a lifelong love of learning.

Fiction
Informational Text
Persuasive Text
Poetry
Biography
Drama
Media

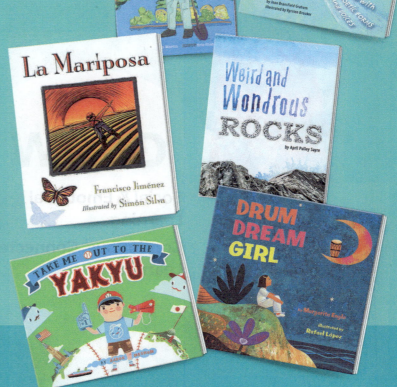

BUILD...

Foundational Skills

Rely on a curriculum that adheres to the **science-based methods** that have proven how students acquire reading skills. **Explicit and systematic instruction** aligned with a **research-based scope and sequence** provides students with a foundation to become confident, independent readers and writers.

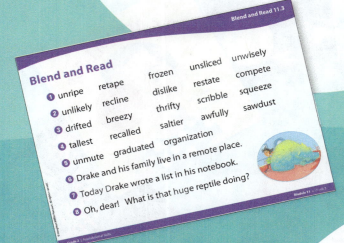

Topic Knowledge & Vocabulary

Systematically build students' understanding of **meaningful topics** and **academic vocabulary**.

Topics and **text sets** are thoughtfully sequenced to build knowledge—like pieces of a puzzle—**within a module, within a grade,** and **across the program**.

Develop Critical and Strategic Thinking Skills

Reading Comprehension

With adequate decoding skills, students have the building blocks they need to **comprehend** what they read.

Teach students to recognize **genre characteristics**, **cite text evidence**, and draw from a growing bank of **skills** and **strategies** to make meaning from complex grade-level texts.

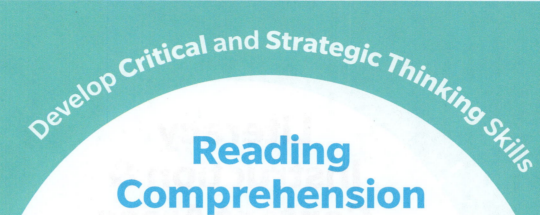

- PHONOLOGICAL AWARENESS
- PHONICS/DECODING
- FLUENCY
- VOCABULARY
- COMPREHENSION

CONNECT...

Literacy Instruction & Content Areas

Literacy instruction provides the "how" for what students learn in **science, social studies, the arts,** and more.

As students read and talk about texts, they will naturally **build background and knowledge** about grade-level **cross-curricular topics** and **standards**.

Student Choice & Independent Practice

The **power of choice** can be motivating, and what is interesting to one student may not appeal to another.

Access **meaningful independent work** and a wide variety of **relevant, rich, authentic texts** for independent reading to offer students appropriate **ownership** of their learning.

Tap into Students' Interests

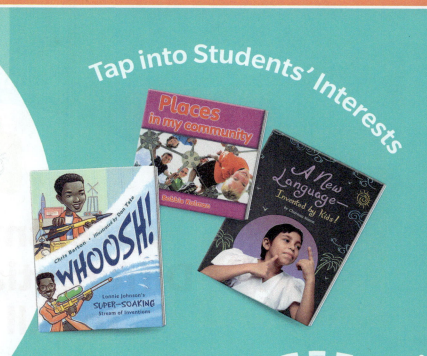

Effective Writing & Communication

Providing daily opportunities for students to **express their understanding and thinking** will help them succeed in today's world.

Support the full range of **writing modes and forms** through the steps of the **writing process**, while also developing students' ability to have **productive, collaborative conversations**.

CONNECT...

Reinforce, extend, and intervene!

Assessment Data & Differentiated Support for All Learners

Connect **assessment insights** with relevant instructional content, tools, and resources to **drive student growth** and narrow the achievement gap.

Select from a variety of program resources in order to meet the needs of all learners.

Continually return to the data and **adjust dynamically** in response to students who make **learning gains** at a different pace.

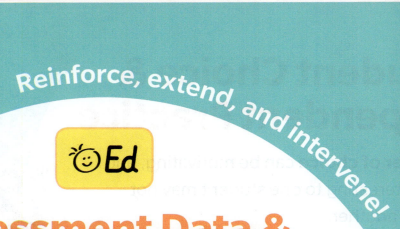

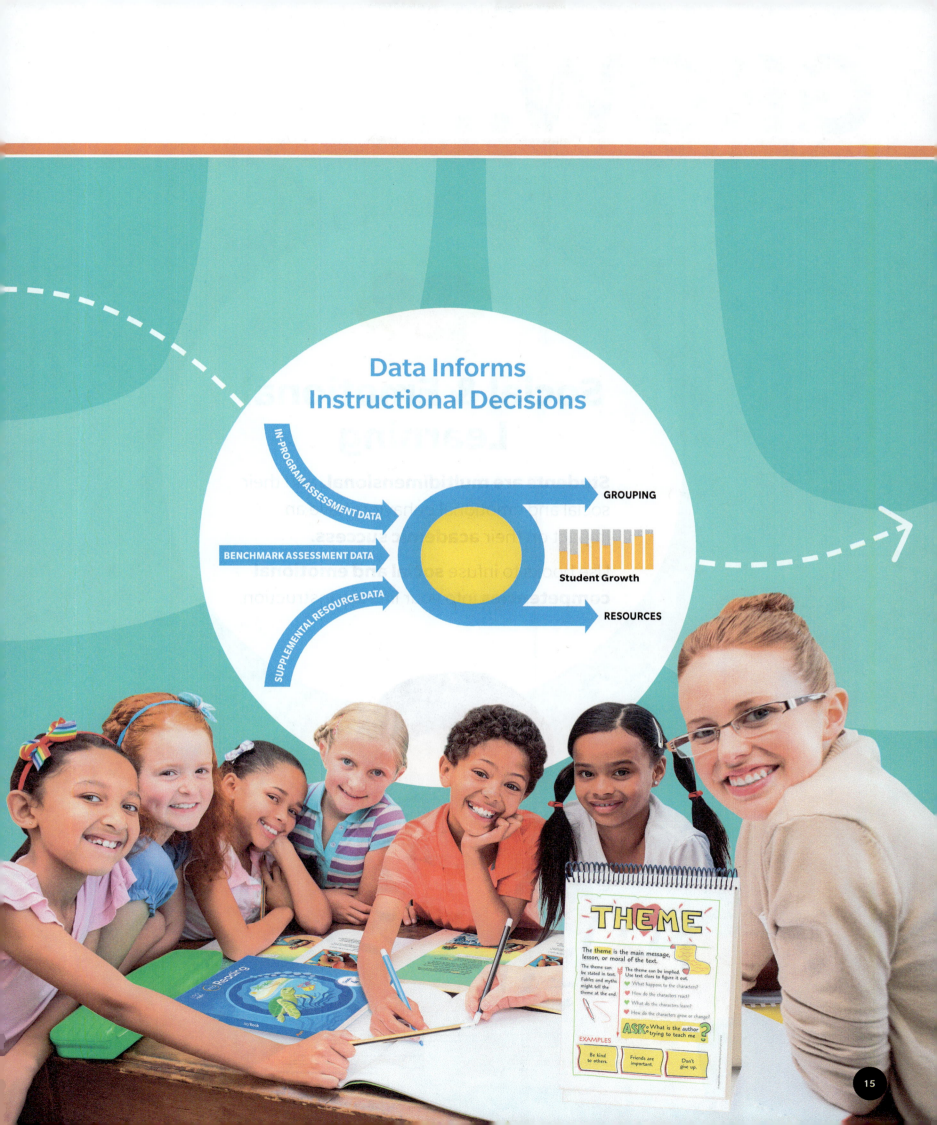

GROW...

Social & Emotional Learning

Students are multidimensional, and their social and emotional behaviors have an impact on their **academic success.**

Use books to infuse **social and emotional competencies** into your literacy instruction.

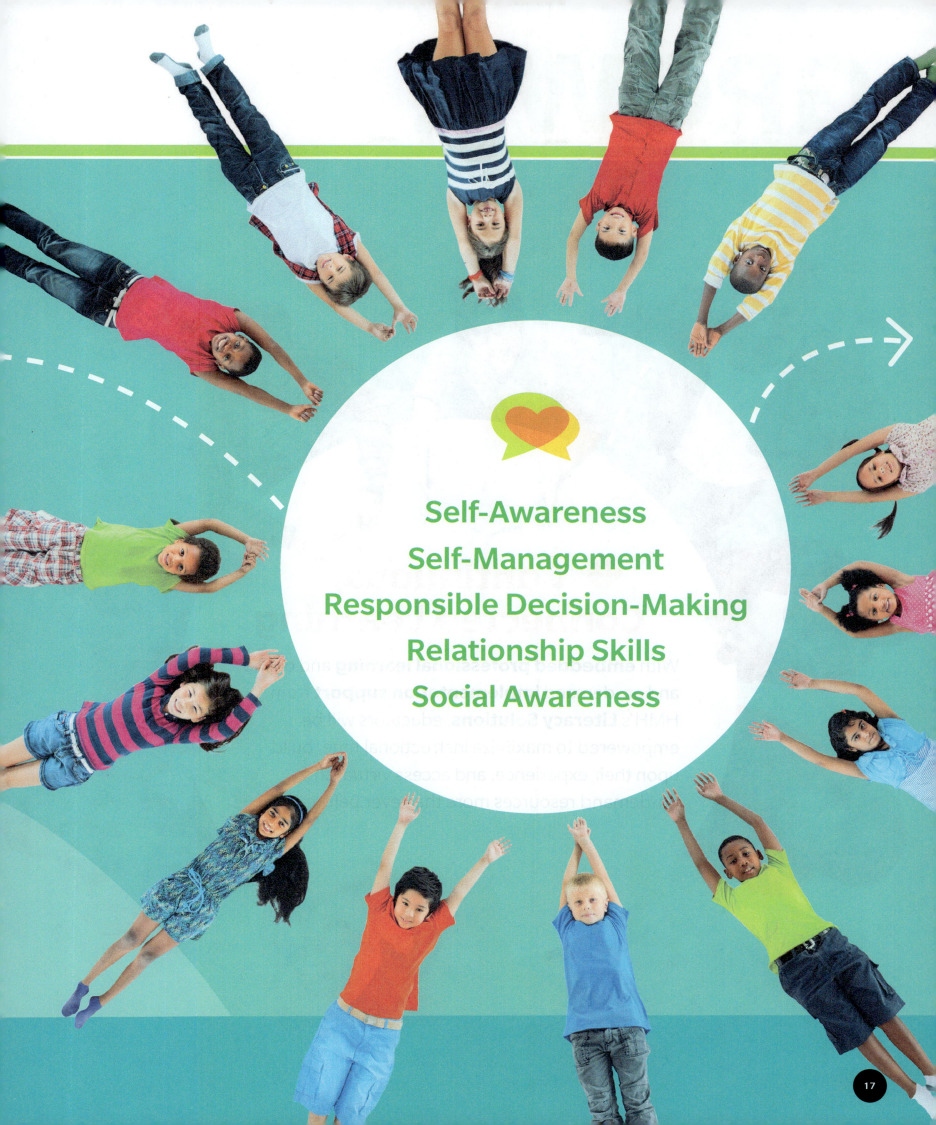

GROW…

We are all continually growing and learning!

Continuous, Connected Learning

With **embedded professional learning** and online and on-demand **implementation support** from HMH's **Literacy Solutions**, educators will be empowered to maximize instructional time, build upon their experience, and access virtual and on-demand resources more than ever before.

Program Tour

Connected Teaching	20
Student and Teacher Resources	22
Year at a Glance	24
Module at a Glance	26
Week at a Glance	28
Connected Teaching with *Ed: Your Friend in Learning*®	32
Grow Your Craft with HMH Literacy Solutions™	34

Program Tour

Connected Teaching

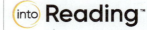

With *HMH Into Reading* and *HMH ¡Arriba la Lectura!*, you and your school will have access to rich content and standards-based instruction, assessments with actionable data insights, professional learning, and supplemental practice and instruction—all connected on the *Ed* learning platform.

With these tools and professional services all within **one seamless experience**, we can ensure you that your students will not only reach their instructional goals, but exceed them.

Comprehensive English Language Arts Program for Kindergarten Through Grade 6

Rich Content and Standards-Based Instruction

- Research-based, explicit, systematic instruction
- Resources and support for whole class, small group, and independent work
- Materials for striving readers and writers, English learners, and advanced learners
- Equitable Spanish Language Arts program, *HMH ¡Arriba la Lectura!*

Assessments and Actionable Data Insights

- Embedded formative assessments
- Growth Measure reports that inform instructional decisions, planning, and grouping
- Ongoing progress monitoring
- Oral reading fluency assessments and dyslexia screening with *HMH Into Reading* content recommendations

PROGRAM TOUR

Supplemental Practice and Instruction

- Personalized, adaptive foundational skills and comprehension skills practice for each student
- On-the-spot corrective feedback
- Embedded assessment
- Optional resources

Professional Learning

- Implementation support: Getting Started for every teacher
- Teacher's Corner: curated, on-demand curriculum-aligned content and teaching support
- Online team coaching tailored to your learning needs

Student and Teacher Resources

STUDENT RESOURCES

WHOLE CLASS

Ed **Student Management Center**
- Access all program materials
- Complete and submit assignments and assessments
- Track progress

*Online-only resource

Grade 1 myBook
5 Books

Grade 2 myBook
3 Books

Read Aloud Books

Big Books
(Grade 1)

TEACHER RESOURCES

Ed **Teacher Management Center**
- Access all program materials
- Plan lessons
- Assign materials
- View assessment reports
- Group students
- Remote learning support

Teacher's Guide
4 Volumes

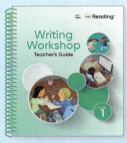
Writing Workshop Teacher's Guide

Anchor Charts*

Daily Show and Teach Slides*

Grade 1 Teaching Pal
5 Books

Grade 2 Teaching Pal
3 Books

Vocabulary Cards

BookStix*

Display and Engage*

*Online-only resource

FOUNDATIONAL SKILLS RESOURCES

Start Right Reader
6 Books

Know It, Show It

Sound/Spelling Cards

Word Cards

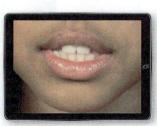
Articulation Videos*

Picture Cards

Letter Cards

OPTIONAL CONNECTED RESOURCES

iRead*

Amira*

PROGRAM TOUR

SMALL-GROUP AND INDEPENDENT APPLICATION

Focal Texts | Writer's Notebook | Know It, Show It | Grammar Practice Workbook | Read and Respond Journal

OPTIONAL CONNECTED RESOURCE

Waggle*

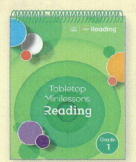
Tabletop Minilessons: Reading

Tabletop Minilessons: English Language Development

Take and Teach Lessons: Leveled Readers

Book Club Discussion Guide

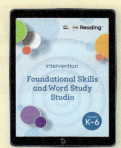
Foundational Skills and Word Study Studio*

ASSESSMENTS

Data & Reporting
- Growth Measure*
- Guided Reading Benchmark Assessment Kit*
- Amira Learning*

Program Assessments
- Module Assessments*
- Weekly Assessments*
- Selection Quizzes*
- Screening, Diagnostic, and Progress-Monitoring*
- Leveled Reader Quizzes*

OPTIONAL CONNECTED RESOURCE

PROFESSIONAL LEARNING & IMPLEMENTATION

Professional Learning Modules and Videos are also provided online.

Program Guide

Teacher's Corner*

Program Tour 23

Year at a Glance

Follow the suggested program timeline to plan instruction and administer assessments throughout the course of the year.

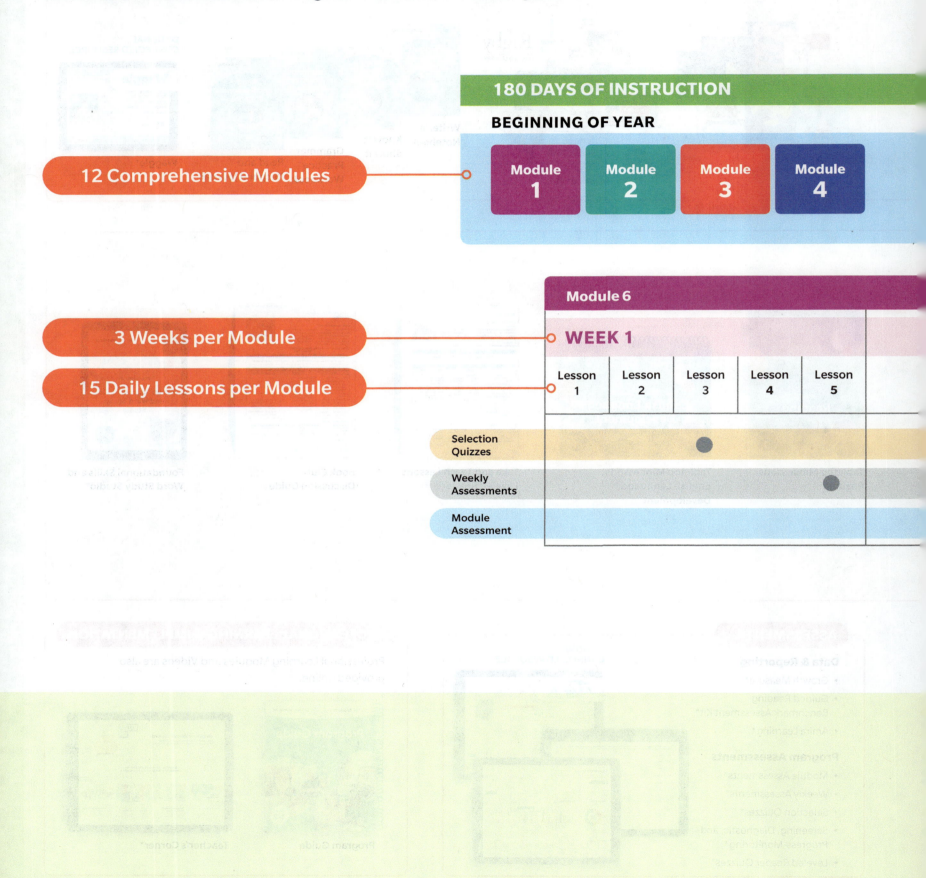

PROGRAM TOUR

MID-YEAR | END OF YEAR

| Module 5 | Module 6 | Module 7 | Module 8 | Module 9 | Module 10 | Module 11 | Module 12 |

WEEK 2					WEEK 3				
Lesson 6	Lesson 7	Lesson 8	Lesson 9	Lesson 10	Lesson 11	Lesson 12	Lesson 13	Lesson 14	Lesson 15
	●		●		●				
			●						●
									●

Program Tour 25

Module at a Glance

MODULE PLANNING

PREVIEW your **three-week module** that focuses on a **high-interest topic**, which children explore through literature and media in **different genres**.

NOTE **skills and texts** that you will cover each week.

Teacher's Guide

MODULE LAUNCH

INTRODUCE the module's **knowledge-building focus** and **build background**.

WATCH a **Get Curious Video** to spark interest in the module topic.

DISCUSS a few **Big Idea Words** about the topic, and have children complete a Vocabulary Network.

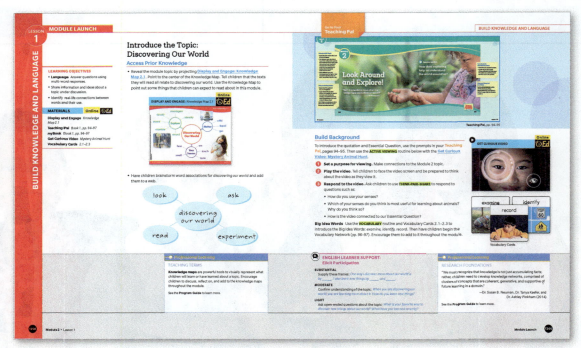

Teacher's Guide

26 Program Guide • Grades 1–2

> **FIND OUT MORE** See the **Teaching and Learning** section to take a deeper dive into the planning supports, research-based instructional design, and program routines.

PROGRAM TOUR

MODULE WRAP-UP

GUIDE children to **synthesize and connect** what they learned about the module topic.

ASSIGN a **culminating performance task** that asks children to demonstrate understanding of topic knowledge and **cite evidence** from the texts they read.

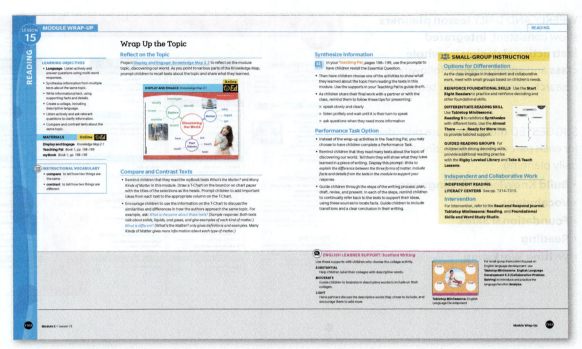

Teacher's Guide

INQUIRY AND RESEARCH

HAVE **collaborative groups** complete an **inquiry and research project** related to the module topic, paced over the three-week module.

SUPPORT children with **conducting research** and **organizing information** about the topic to **present**.

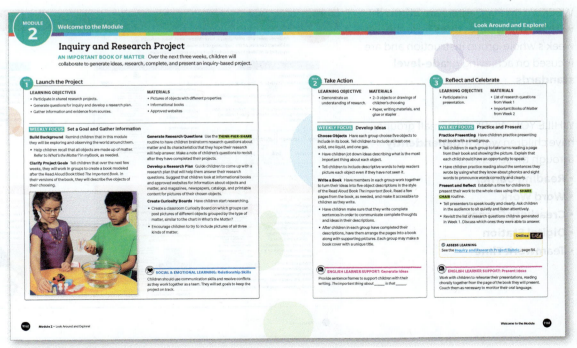

Teacher's Guide

Program Tour 27

Week at a Glance

WEEKLY PLANNING

WEEKLY AND DAILY **lesson planners** show consistent, **integrated instructional design** for **whole class** and **small groups**, following a research-based scope and sequence.

SUGGESTED **daily times** are provided for each part of the instruction to guide daily planning.

- **Build Knowledge & Language**
- **Vocabulary**
- **Foundational Skills**
- **Reading**
- **Writing Workshop**

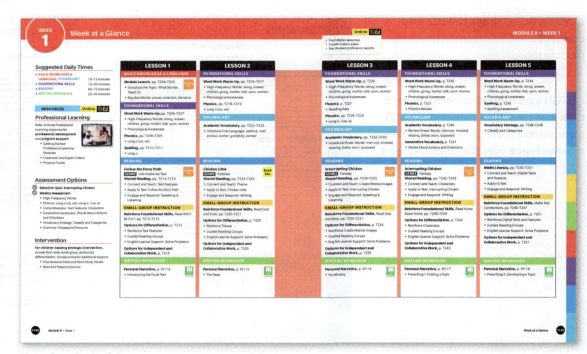

Teacher's Guide

LITERACY CENTERS

WEEKLY Literacy Centers are **aligned with learning objectives** from the week's whole-group instruction and are focused on achieving **grade-level standards**.

WHILE YOU WORK with small groups, have children work **independently** through these centers:

- **Reading Corner**
- **Word Work**
- **Creativity Corner**
- **Digital Station**
- **Teamwork Time**

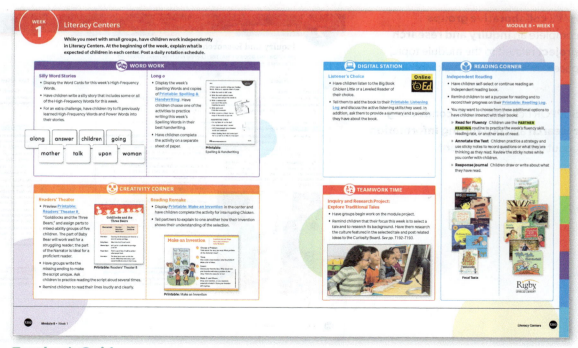

Teacher's Guide

28 *Program Guide* • Grades 1–2

FIND OUT MORE See the **Teaching and Learning** section to take a deeper dive into the planning supports, research-based instructional design, and program routines.

PROGRAM TOUR

FOUNDATIONAL SKILLS

PROVIDE explicit, systematic instruction grounded in the **science of learning** for all the critical foundational skills for your grade, including **phonological awareness**, **phonics**, **fluency**, **high-frequency words**, and **spelling**.

USE the instructional design to **integrate skills** across these areas—for example, connect decoding/encoding and reinforce decoding while practicing fluency.

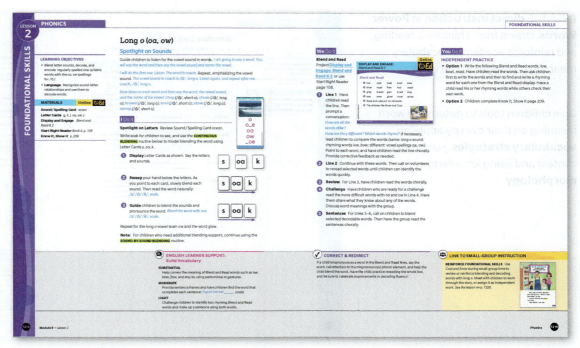

Teacher's Guide

FOUNDATIONAL SKILLS

REINFORCE foundational skills by having children apply them to reading a **decodable text** in their **Start Right Reader**.

CONNECT the decodable texts **related by topic** across a week.

SELECT from **Make Minutes Count** activities to **review** or **provide additional practice** with high-frequency words, phonics, spelling, or handwriting.

Teacher's Guide

Program Tour 29

Week at a Glance

VOCABULARY

PROVIDE **direct instruction** in **Power Words**, drawn from children's reading, and reinforce academic vocabulary meanings throughout the week.

Give children tools to determine word meaning on their own by applying **vocabulary strategies**, such as using context and using knowledge of **morphology**.

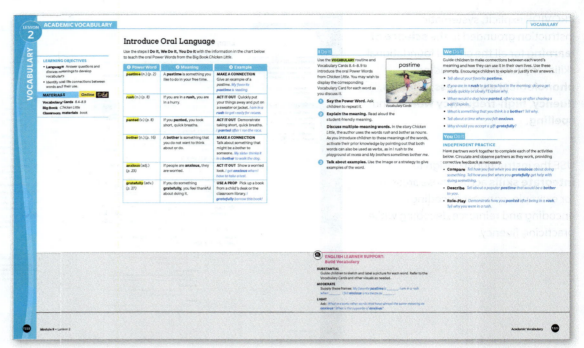

Teacher's Guide

READING

INTRODUCE or review a **comprehension skill** or strategy before reading, using an **Anchor Chart**.

MOVE to your **Teaching Pal** and use the color-coded sticky notes to guide children through **shared reading** and **critical analysis** of a *myBook* text.

- **Blue notes** for first reading to discuss the gist of the text
- **Purple notes** for subsequent readings to gain deeper understanding
- **Red notes** to discuss Notice & Note Signposts

Teacher's Guide

Teaching Pal

30 Program Guide • Grades 1–2

PROGRAM TOUR

WRITING WORKSHOP

FOCUS on a particular **writing mode and form** for a three-week module, guiding children through all the steps of the **writing process**.

HIGHLIGHT aspects of **writer's craft**, using a mentor text.

INTEGRATE instruction for **grammar/conventions** in the context of writing instruction.

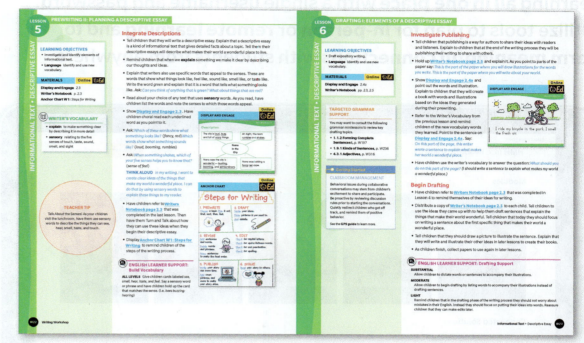

Writing Workshop Teacher's Guide

OPTIONS FOR DIFFERENTIATION

CHOOSE from a variety of **flexible options** to meet children's needs for targeted support in small groups.
- reinforce foundational skills with Start Right Readers
- skill and strategy groups
- English learner groups
- guided reading groups

INTERVENE with children who are below grade level.
- Foundational Skills and Word Study Studio
- Read and Respond Journal

ADJUST your **small groups** frequently in response to data and student growth.

Tabletop Minilessons: English Language Development

Tabletop Minilessons: Reading

Read and Respond Journal

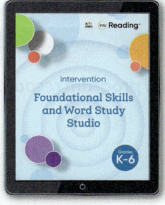

Foundational Skills and Word Study Studio

Program Tour 31

Connected Teaching with Ed, your friend in learning

Use *Ed,* the HMH learning platform, to access core content, assessments, supplemental programs, and curated professional learning **all in one place** with a single username and password. Utilize tools to plan for **in-person** or **remote learning** and to **form meaningful connections** with students from anywhere.

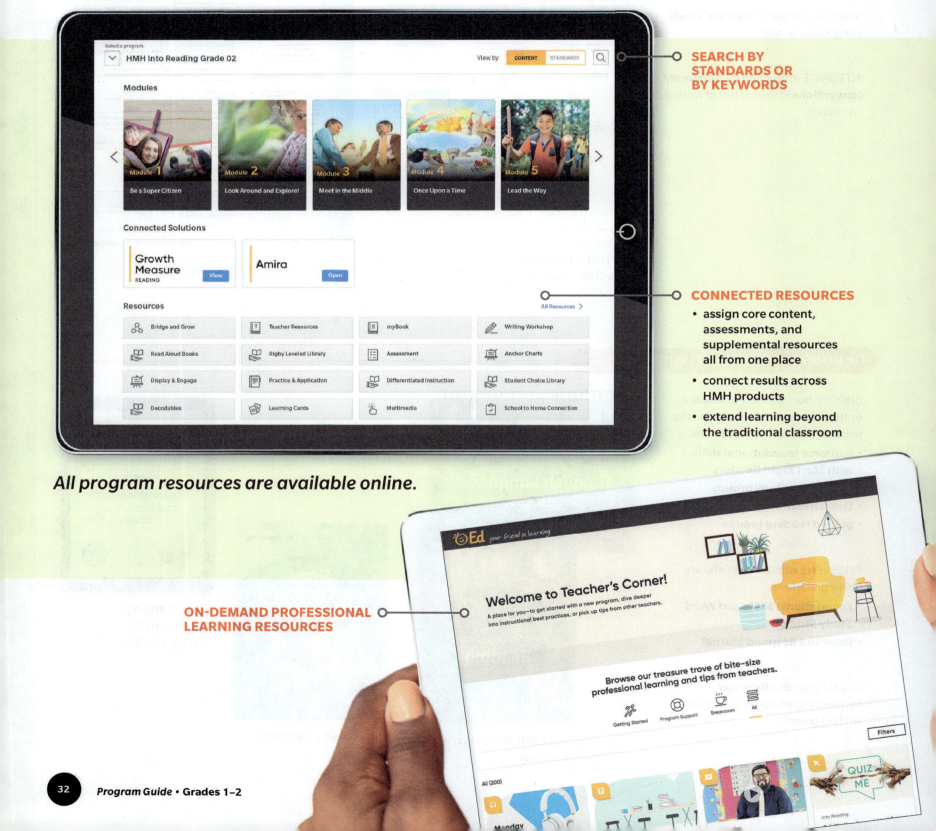

All program resources are available online.

SEARCH BY STANDARDS OR BY KEYWORDS

CONNECTED RESOURCES
- assign core content, assessments, and supplemental resources all from one place
- connect results across HMH products
- extend learning beyond the traditional classroom

ON-DEMAND PROFESSIONAL LEARNING RESOURCES

Program Guide • Grades 1–2

PROGRAM TOUR

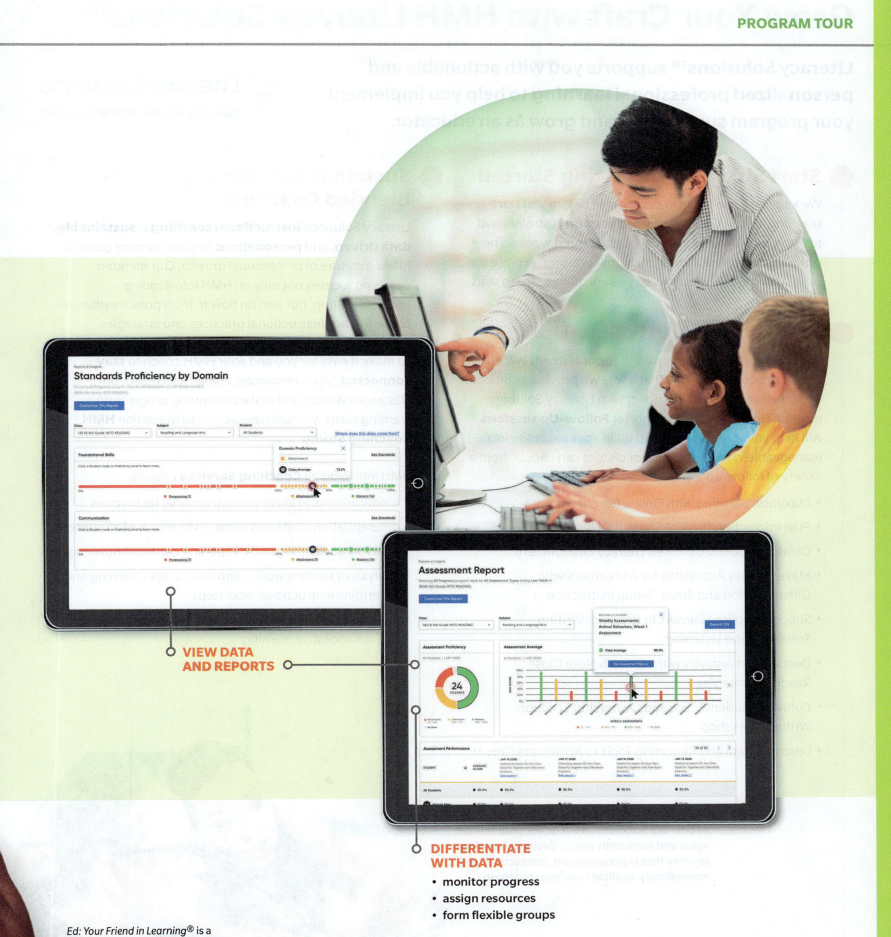

VIEW DATA AND REPORTS

DIFFERENTIATE WITH DATA
- monitor progress
- assign resources
- form flexible groups

Ed: Your Friend in Learning® is a registered trademark of Houghton Mifflin Harcourt.

Program Tour 33

Grow Your Craft with HMH Literacy Solutions™

Literacy Solutions™ supports you with actionable and personalized professional learning to help you implement your program successfully and grow as an educator.

🔸 Start Strong with Getting Started

We know you can't take in every detail before you start teaching, so our **Getting Started session** is streamlined to focus on preparing you for your first three weeks. The **online experience** allows you to follow along, explore the program, and ask questions so you are off to a strong start.

🔸 Stay Strong with Follow-Up

As expected, more questions and support needs will arise once you begin teaching. That's why we provide additional opportunities for you to connect with Literacy Solutions throughout the year. These shorter **Follow-Up sessions** will help you stay engaged and build your expertise in a manageable way. Your school or district can choose from a variety of follow-up topics, including:

- Maximize Learning with Online Resources
- Plan Instruction to Meet Students' Needs
- Create a Student-Centered Literacy Environment
- Make Literacy Accessible for All Learners with Differentiation and Small-Group Instruction
- Support English Learners in Reading, Writing, Speaking, and Listening
- Deepen Text Analysis with Notice & Note Close Reading Strategies
- Cultivate Student Voice and Ownership Through Writing Workshop
- Leverage Data and Reporting Tools to Accelerate Growth

At Literacy Solutions, we'll honor your unique voice and work with you to design a learning journey that is personalized, interactive, and immediately applicable to your teaching.

🔸 Sustain Practices with Blended Coaching

Literacy Solutions **instructional coaching** is **sustainable**, **data driven**, and **personalized** to your learning goals to foster a culture of professional growth. Our blended coaching focuses not only on *HMH Into Reading* implementation, but also on how to incorporate evidence-based literacy instructional practices and strategies.

To make it easy for you and your HMH coach to **stay connected**, share resources, upload and reflect on classroom videos, and make continuing progress on learning goals, you will have access to the online **HMH Coaching Studio**.

HMH Into Reading **Coaching Services** provide

- model lessons to illustrate instructional techniques
- differentiation strategies to meet the needs of all students
- focus on developing and deepening content knowledge
- analysis of student work samples to assess learning and determine instructional next steps
- facilitation of professional learning communities, cadres, and collaborative learning

PROGRAM TOUR

Support at Your Fingertips Through Teacher's Corner

We want you to feel confident teaching with *HMH Into Reading*. **Teacher's Corner** on *Ed: Your Friend in Learning*® gives you the support you want with an ever-growing library of **professional learning resources**—from **authentic class videos** to **tips from other teachers** and our **team of experienced coaches**.

Whether you want to quickly prep for a lesson or invest time in your own professional growth, we have **on-demand trusted resources** to enhance your instruction today.

Teacher's Corner

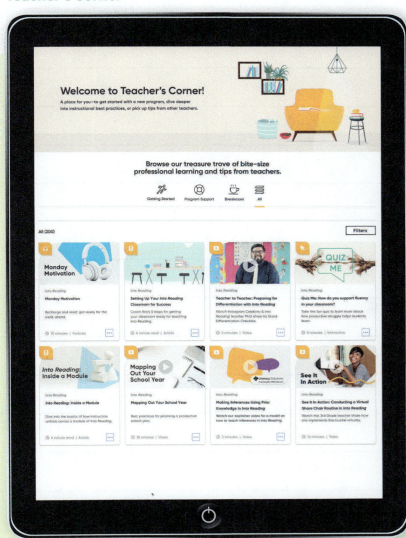

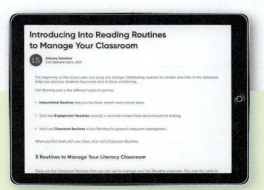

ON DEMAND, BUT NOT ONE-SIZE-FITS-ALL

Choose from bite-size professional learning resources designed to be easily applicable to tomorrow's instruction.

CURATED, TRUSTED CONTENT

There's no shortage of free resources online, but with Teacher's Corner, professional learning and instructional recommendations align to best practices. Hear from thought leaders, experienced coaches, and practicing teachers.

Notes

Teaching and Learning

Teaching and Learning

PLANNING AND PACING
Planning Made Easy 38
Scheduling and Remote Teaching Support 40
Implement Effective Classroom Routines.......... 42

BUILD KNOWLEDGE AND LANGUAGE
Knowledge Networks................................. 44

FOUNDATIONAL SKILLS
Phonological Awareness 46
Phonics and Fluency................................. 48
Spelling and Handwriting........................... 50
High-Frequency Words.............................. 52

ORAL LANGUAGE AND VOCABULARY
Academic Vocabulary................................ 54
Generative Vocabulary and Vocabulary Strategies ... 56
Speaking and Listening 58

READING
Text Sets and Text Complexity 60
Comprehension Skills and Strategies 62
Dialogic Reading with Read Alouds 64
Shared Reading 66
Writing in Response to Texts 68
Independent Reading 70

OPTIONS FOR DIFFERENTIATION
Small-Group Instruction 72

WRITING WORKSHOP
Writing Process 74
Grammar... 76

RESEARCH
Inquiry and Research 78

Research Foundations............................... 80

Teaching and Learning

PLANNING AND PACING
Planning Made Easy

Use the program **planning supports** to suit your needs, whether you intend to use the modules sequentially as designed or to teach by standard according to a school or district framework.

Teach by Module

HMH Into Reading provides daily lesson plans for 180 days of instruction, including whole-class, small-group, and independent work. Literacy experts informed the research-based scope and sequence to accomplish these goals:

- **organize text sets** into modules based on meaningful content-area topics
- **integrate** the essential early literacy skills: phonological awareness, phonics/decoding, fluency, vocabulary, and comprehension
- **progress** from simple to more complex texts and skills throughout the year and review skills cumulatively

Ed Access each grade's **Foundational Skills Scope and Sequence** and a complete **grade-level Scope and Sequence** online.

SUGGESTED TIMES
Suggested Daily Times provide a range of time for each literacy strand to guide planning and adapt to your schedule.

MAKE CONNECTIONS
Clear sequence of instruction makes meaningful connections between vocabulary, reading, writing, and foundational skills.

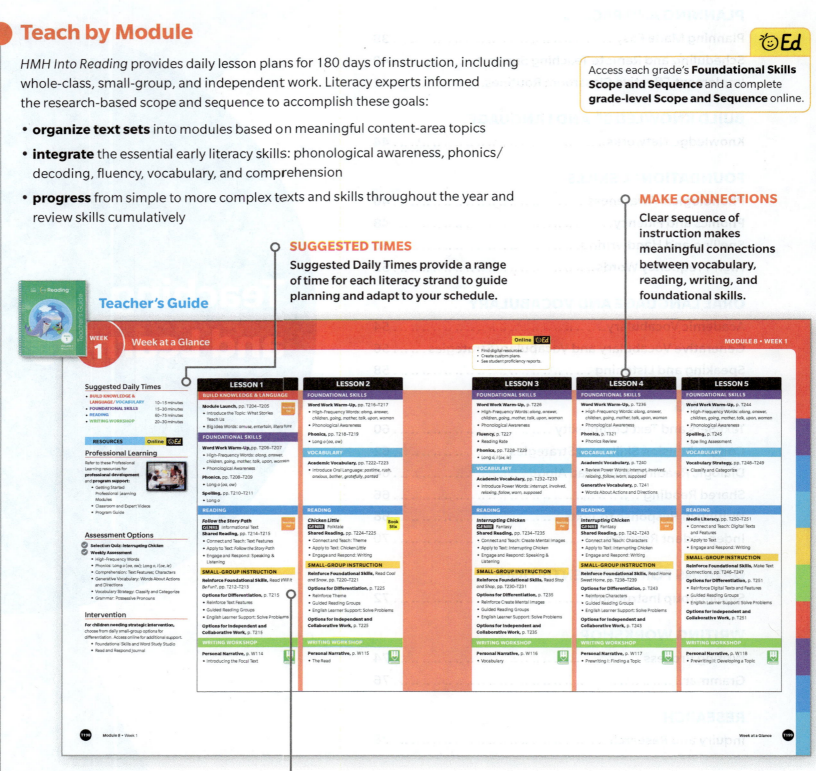

FLEXIBLE OPTIONS
Flexible daily options for small-group differentiation help teachers make instructional decisions based on student data and observation.

38 Program Guide • Grades 1–2

TEACHING AND LEARNING

Teach by Standard or Skill

Ed: Your Friend in Learning provides tools for flexible customization of *HMH Into Reading* to meet your needs.

PREVIEW AND BROWSE
Preview and browse the modules and resources in the program module carousel, or view by resource category.

CREATE LESSON PLANS
Create lesson plans for your own customized units. Lesson plans can become your shortcut to the resources you want to use.

VIEW OR SEARCH
View or search by standard to identify resources that align with your instructional goals.

SEARCH BY SKILL
Search by skill by typing the skill name into the search field.

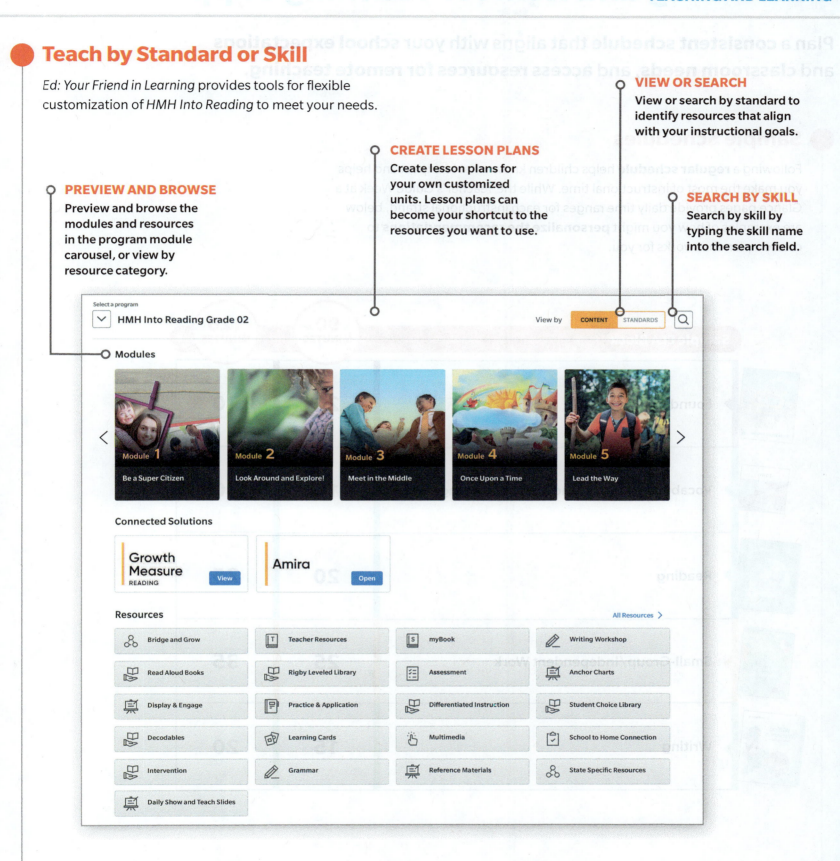

* Note about Foundational Skills: HMH strongly recommends using the Foundational Skills sequentially as designed in the program's Foundational Skills Scope and Sequence. Phonics/decoding skills build cumulatively, so children will experience their maximum reading gains if they receive direct instruction in all the skills in a developmentally appropriate sequence.

PLANNING AND PACING
Scheduling and Remote Teaching Support

Plan a **consistent schedule** that aligns with your **school expectations** and **classroom needs**, and **access resources for remote teaching**.

Sample Schedules

Following a **regular schedule** helps children know what to expect and helps you make the most of instructional time. While the Teacher's Guide Week at a Glance pages provide daily time ranges for each instructional strand, below are examples of how you might **personalize the recommendations** to create a plan that works for you.

Sample ELA Block	90 MINUTES	120 MINUTES
Foundational Skills	20	30
Vocabulary or Build Knowledge and Language	10	10
Reading	20	25
Small-Group/Independent Work	25	35
Writing	15	20

40 *Program Guide • Grades 1–2*

TEACHING AND LEARNING

Support for Remote Teaching

Having the right resources to teach remotely is more important now than ever. *HMH Into Reading* offers a variety of resources to help you meet this challenge and enhance your in-person teaching resources, too.

BRIDGE AND GROW PATHWAYS

Bridge and Grow Pathways is a toolkit that complements *HMH Into Reading* to support teachers with some of today's most critical needs: remote teaching, student learning loss, effective use of technology, and students' social and emotional learning needs.

Included in this toolkit is **HMH Priority Standards Pathways**, a guide to help teachers focus on the most important areas of instruction, as well as a curated set of recommended resources for teaching, practice and application, and formative assessment aligned to the Priority Standards.

DAILY SHOW AND TEACH SLIDES

Daily Show and Teach Slides facilitate seamless lesson delivery, either remotely or in-class, with all of a lesson's resources pulled together in a student-facing slide show. Instructional support notes and model language on each slide guide teachers through successful implementation with little to no preparation. This resource is available in English and Spanish.

TEACHER'S CORNER

Teacher's Corner on *Ed: Your Friend in Learning* is an ever-growing library of bite-size professional learning resources, from authentic class videos to tips from other teachers and our team of experienced coaches. Relevant support and tips for remote teaching best practices are included among the resources.

Daily Show and Teach Slides

Bridge and Grow Pathways

Teacher's Corner

Teaching and Learning 41

Implement Effective Classroom Routines

Use researched-based routines to target the **acquisition of key skills**, support effective **classroom management**, and strategically structure **student engagement** so that all children are actively participating, thinking, and responding.

Routine Types at a Glance

See Teacher's Guide Volume 1, p. R9, to access the steps for all of the routines, learn why they are important, and get support for implementation.

INSTRUCTIONAL ROUTINES

Instructional routines embedded throughout *HMH Into Reading* support children in learning new skills. Consistent, familiar routines allow children to focus on the learning rather than the steps for a new activity, while also supporting your lesson planning.

- ACTIVE VIEWING
- VOCABULARY
- HIGH-FREQUENCY WORDS
- BLENDING: SOUND-BY-SOUND BLENDING (GRADE 1 ONLY)
- BLENDING: CONTINUOUS BLENDING
- BLENDING: VOWEL-FIRST BLENDING (GRADE 1 ONLY)
- SYLLABICATION: VCCV PATTERN
- SYLLABICATION: VCV PATTERN (GRADE 2 ONLY)
- SYLLABICATION: VCCCV PATTERN (GRADE 2 ONLY)

ENGAGEMENT ROUTINES

Engagement routines help to create a safe classroom environment in which all children feel comfortable participating and engaging in their learning. When consistently applied, these routines will help you determine whether particular children need additional support.

- TURN AND TALK
- THINK-PAIR-SHARE
- WRITE AND REVEAL
- SHARE CHAIR
- ECHO READING
- CHORAL READING
- PARTNER READING
- PICK AND POINT

CLASSROOM MANAGEMENT ROUTINES

Classroom management routines help all children follow expectations, focus on productive learning, and build confidence and independence. They also establish norms for smooth transitions and help to reduce disruptions.

- QUIET CUE
- SILENT SIGNALS
- GIVE ME FIVE!
- ASK THREE, THEN ME
- PARTNER UP

TEACHING AND LEARNING

• Embedded Support

All of the program routines are highlighted within the Teacher's Guide lessons and serve to build structure and continuity between lessons.

Teacher's Guide

LOCATE ROUTINES
Look for routines highlighted in GREEN.

LESSON 2 — PHONICS

FOUNDATIONAL SKILLS

Long o (oa, ow)

Spotlight on Sounds

Guide children to listen for the vowel sound in words. *I am going to say a word. You will say the word and then say the vowel sound and name the vowel.*

I will do the first one. Listen: The word is coach. Repeat, emphasizing the vowel sound. *The vowel sound in coach is /ō/, long o. Listen again, and repeat after me:* coach, /ō/, long o.

Now listen to each word and then say the word, the vowel sound, and the name of the vowel: chop (/ŏ/, short o); chose (/ō/, long o); known (/ō/, long o); knot (/ŏ/, short o); stove (/ō/, long o); stomp (/ŏ/, short o).

LEARNING OBJECTIVES
- Blend letter sounds, decode, and encode regularly spelled one-syllable words with the *oa, ow* spellings for /ō/.
- **Language** Recognize sound-letter relationships and use them to decode words.

MATERIALS — Online Ed
Sound/Spelling Card ocean
Letter Cards g, k, l, oa, ow, s
Display and Engage Blend and Read 8.2
Start Right Reader Book 4, p. 108
Know It, Show It p. 209

I Do It

Spotlight on Letters Review Sound/Spelling Card *ocean*. Write *soak* for children to see, and use the **CONTINUOUS BLENDING** routine below to model blending the word using Letter Cards *s, oa, k*.

1. **Display** Letter Cards as shown. Say the letters and sounds.

   [s] [oa] [k]

2. **Sweep** your hand below the letters. As you point to each card, slowly blend each sound. Then read the word naturally: /s//ō//k/, soak.

   [s] [oa] [k]

3. **Guide** children to blend the sounds and pronounce the word. *Blend the word with me:* /s//ō//k/, soak.

   [s] [oa] [k]

Repeat for the long o vowel team *ow* and the word *glow*.

Note: For children who need additional blending support, continue using the **SOUND-BY-SOUND BLENDING** routine.

STEP IT OUT
Preview the consistent routine steps and model language before teaching a lesson. Instructional routines are stepped out right in the lesson. Find the others in the Resources section of your Teacher's Guide, Volume 1.

EL ENGLISH LEARNER SUPPORT: Build Vocabulary

SUBSTANTIAL
Help convey the meaning of Blend and Read words such as *low, blow, flow,* and *stay* by using pantomime or gestures.

MODERATE
Provide sentence frames and have children find the word that completes each sentence: *A goat can eat _____.* (oats)

LIGHT
Challenge children to identify two rhyming Blend and Read words and make up a sentence using both words.

T218 Module 8 • Lesson 2

Teaching and Learning 43

BUILD KNOWLEDGE AND LANGUAGE
Knowledge Networks

Help children **build networks of knowledge** so that they can construct meaning as they read.

 Why It Matters

Wide and deep knowledge of a range of meaningful topics is central to reading success and enables children to become effective members of their communities. When literacy instruction is **structured to build knowledge systematically** over time, children will be more likely to comprehend what they are reading—in other words, they will continually build on what they already know to become better readers and communicators.

A **knowledge network** is a set of interconnected ideas that work together to build knowledge. As children learn new concepts, they can use knowledge networks to

- **build schema**, connecting new ideas to existing ones
- **map ideas** onto a web of knowledge in order to make sense of them and hold them in their memory

Each three-week module is focused on a central topic, which children explore through carefully curated texts, media, and projects. Topics are developed and expanded within and across grades.

Use the **Introduce the Topic** lessons in the Teacher's Guide to launch each module. Continually return to a **Knowledge Map** throughout the module as children encounter new texts and media about the topic. At the end of the module, guide children to **synthesize** what they learned and complete a culminating task. *For a complete list of module topics and texts, see pp. 144–151.*

TEACHING AND LEARNING

Teacher's Guide

ACCESS PRIOR KNOWLEDGE
Use prompts to spark children's interest, introduce the module topic, and discuss a quotation and the Essential Question.

BUILD BACKGROUND
View and discuss a Get Curious Video to begin building topic knowledge.

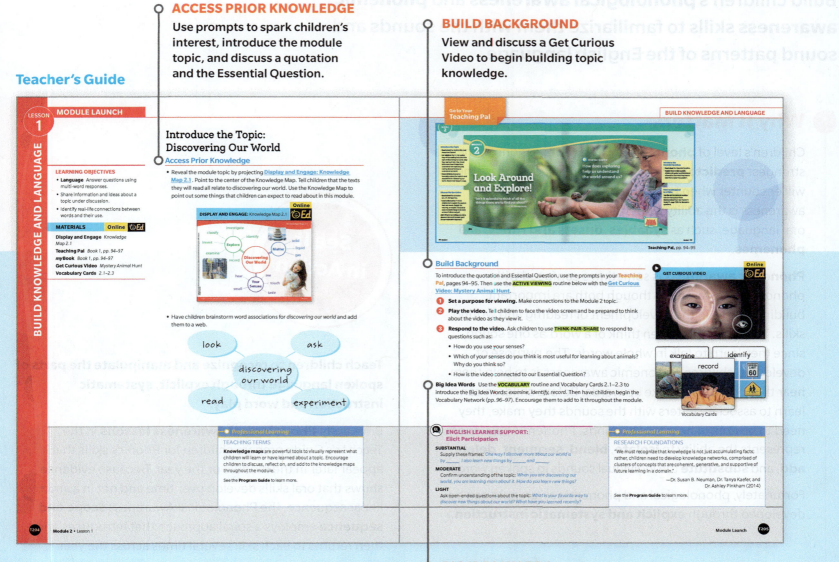

BIG IDEA WORDS
Introduce and discuss words about the topic.

KNOWLEDGE FOCUS
Display and discuss a Knowledge Map to establish a knowledge focus and facilitate making connections between texts.

Display and Engage

Teaching and Learning

FOUNDATIONAL SKILLS
Phonological Awareness

Build children's **phonological awareness** and **phonemic awareness** skills to familiarize them with the sounds and sound patterns of the English language.

Why It Matters

Children's level of **phonological awareness** is one of the strongest **predictors** of the success or lack of success they will encounter when beginning to read. Phonological awareness is the ability to identify and manipulate units of oral language, such as **syllables**, **onsets and rimes**, and **phonemes**.

Phonemic awareness is sometimes confused with phonological awareness, though both are important building blocks in the development of reading and writing skills. Young children often think of a word as one sound, since they learn to talk in whole words. The purpose of developing children's phonemic awareness is to help them hear the sounds that make up words. Before children can learn to associate letters with the sounds they make, they need to be able to hear those sounds. Phonemic awareness represents the ability to **isolate**, **blend**, **segment**, **delete**, **add**, and **substitute** the individual sounds in spoken words.

Fortunately, phonological and phonemic awareness can be developed through **explicit and systematic instruction**.

See It in Action

Teach children to recognize and manipulate the parts of spoken language through explicit, systematic instruction and word play.

Brief **daily Phonological Awareness lessons** in the Teacher's Guide prepare children for Phonics skills that appear later in the module or the year. Because evidence shows that oral skills develop over time and not in a strict linear sequence, the Phonological Awareness **scope and sequence** employs a spiral approach that introduces and then returns to each skill several times across the year.

In addition, an oral warm-up to introduce each Phonics lesson, labeled **Spotlight on Sounds**, provides review of a phonemic awareness skill right before a related Phonics skill is introduced.

Spanish Foundational Skills
See the *¡Arriba la Lectura!* section to learn about the program's equitable and authentic approach to teaching Spanish foundational skills.

TEACHING AND LEARNING

MODEL LANGUAGE
Refer to model language to introduce each skill and prompt children to apply it.

Teacher's Guide

FOUNDATIONAL SKILLS

Phonological Awareness

Blend Phonemes

- Remind children that they can blend sounds, or phonemes, to say words.
- Use word pairs with minimal contrasts as you model blending phonemes. Hold up Picture Cards *slide*, *swing*, and *switch* as you say each word.
- Say: *Let's see how well you can blend sounds to say words. Listen to these sounds: /s/ /l/ /ī/ /d/. If I blend the sounds, I will say a word. Listen: /s/ /l/ /ī/ /d/, slide. When I blend /s/ /l/ /ī/ /d/, I say the word slide.*
- *Your turn! Blend these sounds to say a word: /s/ /w/ /ĭ/ /ch/. What is the word?* (switch) *Here is another: /s/ /w/ /ĭ/ /ng/.* (swing) *What sounds in swing and switch are the same?* (the sounds at the beginning: /s/, /w/, /ĭ/) *Which sounds in the words are different?* (the ending sounds: /ng/ and /ch/)

- Display Picture Cards *hive*, *lock*, and *nest*.
- Say: *Let's keep practicing. I will say the sounds. Blend the sounds to say the word. If there is a Picture Card, point to the Picture Card as you say the word. Ready? /h/ /ī/ /v/* (hive), */h/ /ĭ/ /t/* (hit); */l/ /ŏ/ /k/* (lock), */l/ /ō/ /n/* (loan); */n/ /ē/ /t/* (neat), */n/ /ĕ/ /s/ /t/* (nest) Ask children what is the same and different about the sounds in each pair of words. As needed, guide them to listen for and note differences in the vowel sounds of the words in each pair.
- For further practice, have children blend the sounds in the names of one-syllable classroom objects, such as these: */d/ /ĕ/ /s/ /k/* (desk), */b/ /ă/ /g/* (bag), */f/ /l/ /ă/ /g/* (flag). Children should point to the correct objects as they blend the word.

STUDENT ENGAGEMENT
Lessons have a lively, engaging pace and varying activity types to maintain children's interest.

USE PICTURES
Use Picture Cards to help children work with sounds without connecting the sounds to letters.

(EL) ENGLISH LEARNER SUPPORT: Build Vocabulary

SUBSTANTIAL
Point out classroom objects that children name at the end of blending. Point to the object, say the name, and have children repeat the name.

MODERATE
Have children complete simple sentences about the objects. *There is a book on my _____.* (desk) *This _____ is green.* (bag)

LIGHT
Ask children to complete sentence frames to explain the location of each object in the classroom. *The flag is _____. My bag is _____.*

✓ CORRECT & REDIRECT
Guide children who have trouble blending sounds in words with minimal contrasts by modeling. Then focus on the vowel sounds.

- Say each sound in the first word and repeat, each time blending the sounds a little more closely together: */n/ /ē/ /t/, /n-ē-t/*, neat. Ask the child to blend and say the word.
- Do the same for the second word in the pair: */n/ /ĕ/ /s/ /t/, /n-e-s-t/*, nest. Ask the child to blend and say the word.
- Now blend the sounds in each word one after the other, focusing on the different vowel sounds: */n/ /ēēē/ /t/*, neat. */n/ /ēēē/ /s/ /t/*, nest. Have the child repeat.

Word Work Warm-Up

ENGLISH LANGUAGE SUPPORT
Build vocabulary for the words on the Picture Cards.

CORRECTIVE FEEDBACK
Correct children's errors immediately, using the provided models.

Teaching and Learning 47

FOUNDATIONAL SKILLS
Phonics and Fluency

Teach children the **critical building blocks** for reading the English language accurately and fluently.

● Why It Matters

Reading research is clear that **explicit and systematic instruction** in foundational reading skills results in improved reading abilities, and it is more effective than acquiring these skills indirectly. This means that the greatest number of children will benefit from phonics instruction that

- adheres to a research-based **scope and sequence**, so that children will not miss any critical sound-spellings in their learning
- follows a **gradual release model** that provides teacher modeling, guided practice, and independent practice

By helping children crack the code of the English language, you will give them the tools they need to experience the thrill of reading connected text fluently—that is, with **accuracy**, **automaticity**, and **appropriate prosody** or **expression**.

See It in Action

Follow the program's scope and sequence, informed by literacy experts, to build and reinforce children's phonics and fluency skills.

The Teacher's Guide includes daily support for **Phonics**. Immediately following **explicit**, **systematic instruction** in whole group, children apply their new phonics skills in the context of engaging **decodable texts**, called Start Right Readers, in small groups. These texts are carefully crafted to offer practice with reading words containing only known phonic elements and high-frequency words.

Weekly **Fluency** lessons feature a spiraling approach that introduces and then returns to each of these skills many times over the course of the year:

- **accuracy and self-correction**
- **reading rate**
- **expression**
- **phrasing**
- **intonation**

Spanish Foundational Skills

See the *¡Arriba la Lectura!* section to learn about the program's equitable and authentic approach to teaching Spanish foundational skills.

Program Guide • Grades 1–2

TEACHING AND LEARNING

WARM-UP
Begin with a phonemic awareness warm-up that relates to the target phonics skill.

GRADUAL RELEASE MODEL
Teach the target sound-spelling, and follow the instructional path in each lesson: I Do It, We Do It, You Do It.

KNOW IT, SHOW IT
Assign Know It, Show It pages for independent practice.

BLENDING PRACTICE
Use Blend and Read lines to have children practice reading words in isolation and in context.

DECODABLE TEXT
Children read decodable text that contains new and previously taught phonic elements daily and also practice fluency.

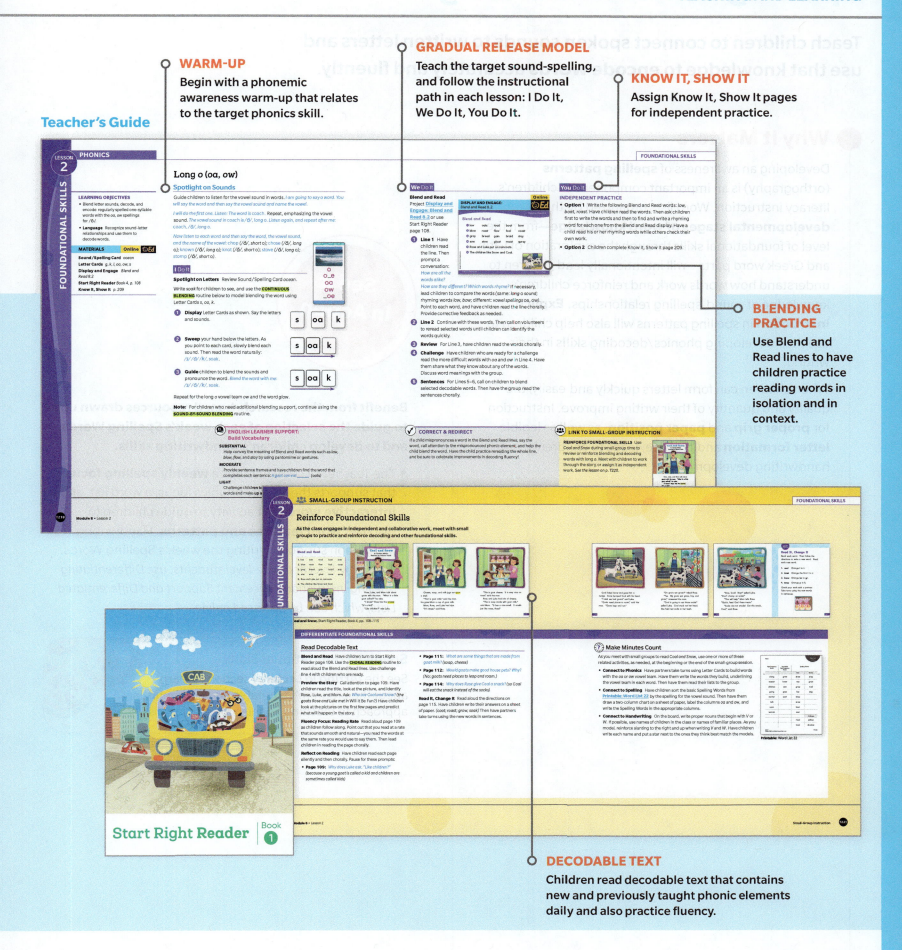

Teaching and Learning 49

FOUNDATIONAL SKILLS
Spelling and Handwriting

Teach children to connect spoken sounds to written letters and use that knowledge to **encode words** accurately and fluently.

● Why It Matters

Developing an awareness of **spelling patterns** (orthography) is an important component of children's literacy instruction. Word lists organized by the **developmental stages of word knowledge**—from the level of foundational skills through the exploration of Latin and Greek word parts—will intentionally lead children to understand how words work and reinforce children's knowledge of sound-spelling relationships. **Explicit instruction** in spelling patterns will also help children to use their developing phonics/decoding skills in their writing.

When children can form letters quickly and easily, the quality and quantity of their writing improve. Instruction for **proper grip** and **paper position**, as well as legible **letter formation** and practice, leads to children's handwriting development.

See It in Action

Benefit from the research-based resources drawn upon to guide the selection of each week's Spelling Words and to develop children's handwriting skills.

- The Teacher's Guide features a **weekly spelling focus** that supports the weekly phonics focus, a word list, and an **interactive word sort** activity to guide children to discover **word features and patterns**. Handwriting instruction supports writing the week's Spelling Words. *For below-level or above-level students, use Differentiating Spelling Instruction: Placement Support and Differentiated Lists, which can be accessed online.*

Spanish Foundational Skills
See the *¡Arriba la Lectura!* section to learn about the program's equitable and authentic approach to teaching Spanish foundational skills.

Program Guide • Grades 1–2

TEACHING AND LEARNING

TEACH THE PRINCIPLE
Provide explicit instruction for the spelling principle. Use Sound/Spelling Cards to support the instruction.

WORD SORT
Model your thinking as you sort a few words by the defined categories in the lesson. Have children complete the word sort and describe the spelling pattern(s).

Teacher's Guide

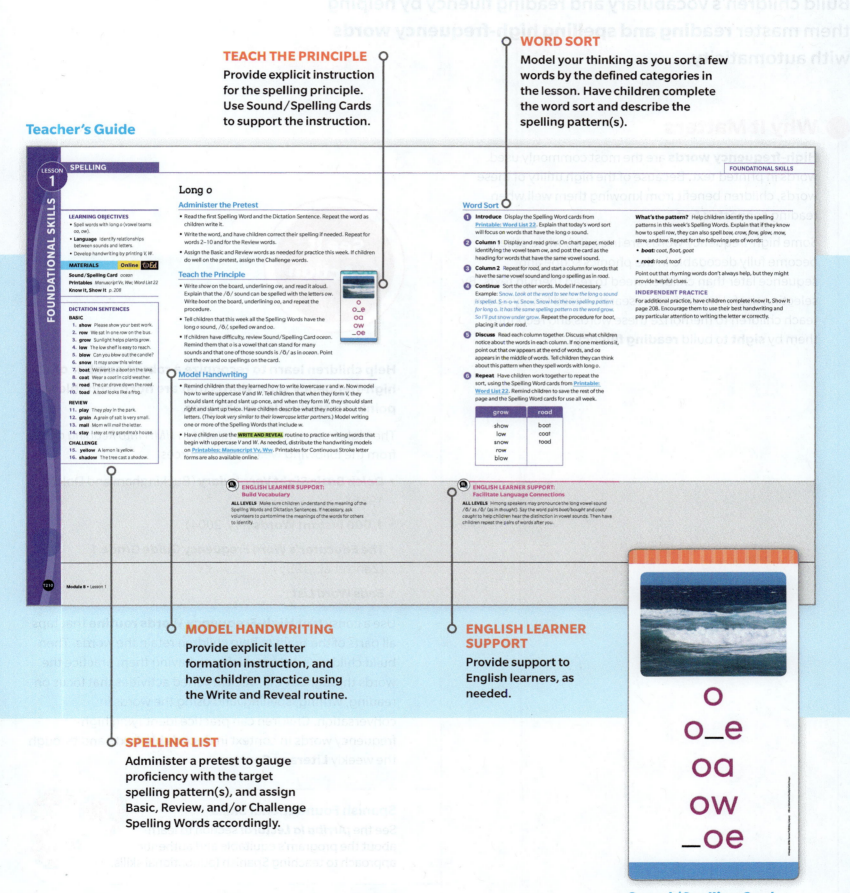

MODEL HANDWRITING
Provide explicit letter formation instruction, and have children practice using the Write and Reveal routine.

ENGLISH LEARNER SUPPORT
Provide support to English learners, as needed.

SPELLING LIST
Administer a pretest to gauge proficiency with the target spelling pattern(s), and assign Basic, Review, and/or Challenge Spelling Words accordingly.

Sound/Spelling Card

Teaching and Learning 51

FOUNDATIONAL SKILLS
High-Frequency Words

Build children's vocabulary and reading fluency by helping them master **reading and spelling high-frequency words with automaticity.**

● Why It Matters

High-frequency words are the most commonly used words in printed text. Because of the high utility of these words, children benefit from knowing them well when reading connected text.

Some high-frequency words are irregular, while others become fully decodable in the phonics scope and sequence later than children need to read them in texts. By selecting useful words from research-based lists, you can teach children to memorize these words and recognize them by **sight** to build **reading fluency**.

See It in Action

Help children learn to recognize a robust number of high-frequency sight words that are not decodable at point of introduction in the year.

The high-frequency words taught in *HMH Into Reading* draw from the following well-known sources:

- ***Dolch Basic Sight Vocabulary*** (Buckingham and Dolch, 1936)
- ***1,000 Instant Words*** (Fry, 2004)
- ***The Educator's Word Frequency Guide Grade 1*** (Zeno et al., 1995)
- ***Eeds Word List***

Use a consistent **High-Frequency Words routine** that taps all parts of the brain to help children retain the words. Then build children's **automaticity** by having them practice the words throughout the week in varied activities that focus on reading, writing, spelling, and using the words in conversation. Children can practice identifying high-frequency words in context in **decodable texts** and through the weekly **Literacy Centers**.

Spanish Foundational Skills
See the *¡Arriba la Lectura!* section to learn about the program's equitable and authentic approach to teaching Spanish foundational skills.

TEACHING AND LEARNING

TEACH THE WORDS
Guide children to see, say, spell, and write the words, using a routine.

Teacher's Guide

LESSON 11

FOUNDATIONAL SKILLS

WORD WORK WARM-UP

LEARNING OBJECTIVES
- Identify and read high-frequency words.
- **Language** Recognize, recite, and write basic sight vocabulary.
- Blend phonemes to say one-syllable words.
- Change phonemes in words to say new words.

MATERIALS Online ⓔEd

Word Cards *brown, few, funny, myself, new, once, thank, words*
Know It, Show It p. 228
Picture Cards *bat (animal), bread, can, chain, duck, goat, lock, rain*

High-Frequency Words
Teach the Words
Use Word Cards *brown, few, funny, myself, new, once, thank,* and *words* and the **HIGH-FREQUENCY WORDS** routine below to introduce the week's High-Frequency sight words.

| brown | few | funny | myself |
| new | once | thank | words |

① **See the word.** Display a Word Card. Say the word, and have children repeat it twice.

② **Say the word.** Have children repeat it chorally. Use the word in a sentence or two. *Thank you for your help. Did you thank Ravi for the gift?* (Use pantomime.)

③ **Spell the word.** Point to the letters, and have children spell the word aloud. Point out any familiar spelling patterns. *Thank ends with k. Can you name something in this room that ends with k?* (desk) *Do you know any other words that end with k?*

④ **Write and check the word.** Hide the word, and have children use the **WRITE AND REVEAL** routine to write the word. Then have them check it against the Word Card.

Have children add this week's words to their individual word rings. Tell them to write a word on the front of each card and write a sentence or draw a picture about the word on the back. Alternatively, you may have children complete Know It, Show It page 228.

INDEPENDENT PRACTICE
Assign a Know It, Show It activity page for children to practice reading and writing the words.

ⓔⓛ ENGLISH LEARNER SUPPORT: Build Vocabulary

ALL LEVELS Use gestures to help reinforce word meanings. For example, pretend to laugh as you say, *That was funny! It made me laugh.* Then have children say *funny* as they repeat the gesture. For the words *brown, few,* and *new,* use or point out classroom objects that can be described using the words.

✓ CORRECT & REDI
Guide children who have tro the correct word, and have
- *Few. What is the word?* (few
- Have children spell the wo word? (few)
- Have children reread all th

---

few ⓘ 126
Review or introduce the vowel sound:
- The letters e-w stand for the long u sound, /yōō/.

Have children blend with you: /f/ /yōō/, *few*.

Sample sentence: *Only a few grapes were left on the stem.*

Word Cards

few

T316 Module 8 • Lesson 11

ENGLISH LEARNER SUPPORT
Use comprehensible input to reinforce word meanings.

Teaching and Learning 53

ORAL LANGUAGE AND VOCABULARY
Academic Vocabulary

Learning flows through language. Provide **direct instruction** with academic vocabulary to **build and expand** children's **word knowledge** within, across, and beyond texts.

● Why It Matters

Having a **rich vocabulary** is critical to future academic success, particularly as texts become increasingly complex through children's schooling. Children with a significant vocabulary gap are at a disadvantage for making gains in their reading development. While some words can be learned from context, many academic vocabulary words require **direct instruction** to build **word awareness** and provide a solid basis for the development of **conceptual knowledge**.

Just as the texts we have children read matter, so do the vocabulary words we teach. Academic vocabulary instruction should focus on words that are

- likely to **boost academic success**
- **relevant to understanding** the texts that children read
- **likely to appear over and over** in other texts

Employ a year-long plan for academic vocabulary development that draws important words from the literature to teach through direct instruction and provides cumulative review to help children retain vocabulary knowledge.

Vocabulary lessons in the Teacher's Guide use a routine approach to introduce each week's **Power Words** and provide meaningful practice in **oral and written contexts**. **Review lessons** appear each week after reading, and **cumulative vocabulary** lessons at the end of each module return to the words again to cement learning over time.

TEACHING AND LEARNING

Teacher's Guide

USE A ROUTINE
Use the Vocabulary routine to introduce Power Words and share each word's student-friendly explanation.

DISCUSS WORDS
Share prompts to discuss and reinforce word meanings in the context of real-world situations.

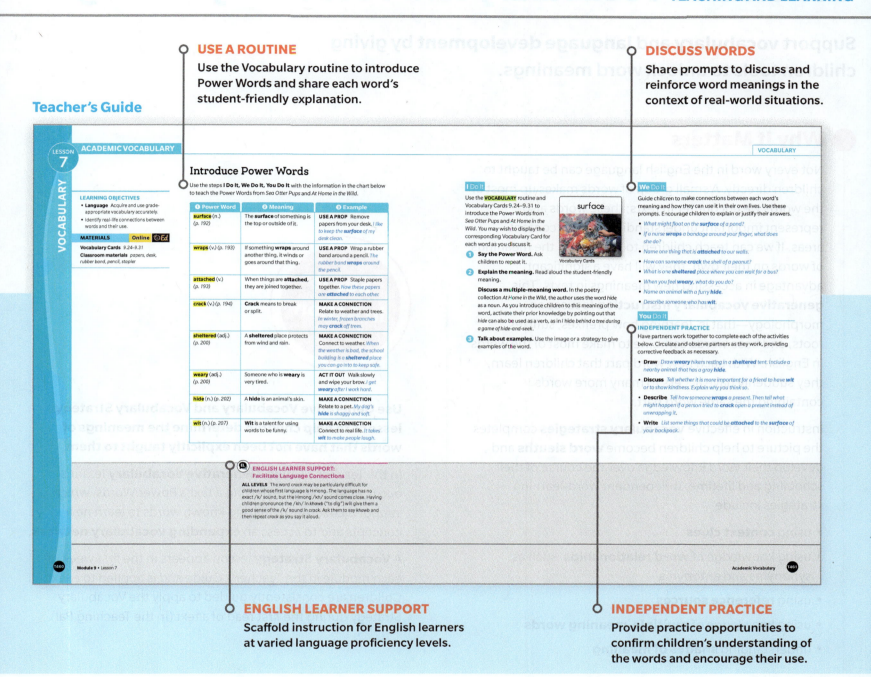

ENGLISH LEARNER SUPPORT
Scaffold instruction for English learners at varied language proficiency levels.

INDEPENDENT PRACTICE
Provide practice opportunities to confirm children's understanding of the words and encourage their use.

Vocabulary Cards

VOCABULARY CARDS
Use images to support word meaning.

Teaching and Learning 55

ORAL LANGUAGE AND VOCABULARY
Generative Vocabulary and Vocabulary Strategies

Support **vocabulary** and **language development** by giving children tools to unlock word meanings.

🔴 Why It Matters

Not every word in the English language can be taught to children directly. A small group of words makes up most of the words we encounter in texts; these words also represent important understandings across content areas. If we can teach children to "generate" the meanings of words on their own, they will have a significant advantage in accessing new meanings in texts. This **generative vocabulary instruction** focuses on morphology—that is, learning how prefixes, suffixes, roots, and base words combine to make most of the words in English. With each new word part that children learn, they suddenly have access to many more words containing the same word part.

Instruction in effective **vocabulary strategies** completes the picture to help children become **word sleuths** and develop their word knowledge over the course of their schooling and lifetime. Independent word-learning strategies include

- using **context clues**
- using knowledge of **word relationships**, such as synonyms and antonyms
- using **reference sources**
- using knowledge of **multiple-meaning words**
- understanding **shades of meaning**

Use Generative Vocabulary and Vocabulary Strategy lessons to help children determine the meanings of words that have not been explicitly taught to them.

In the Teacher's Guide, **Generative Vocabulary** lessons occur weekly, after reviewing a text's Power Words, which supports children in utilizing known words to learn new concepts and to access an **expanding vocabulary network**.

A **Vocabulary Strategy** lesson appears in the first week of each module in the Teacher's Guide and is applied to a text. Children are consistently guided to apply the Vocabulary Strategy during the first read of a text (in the Teaching Pal).

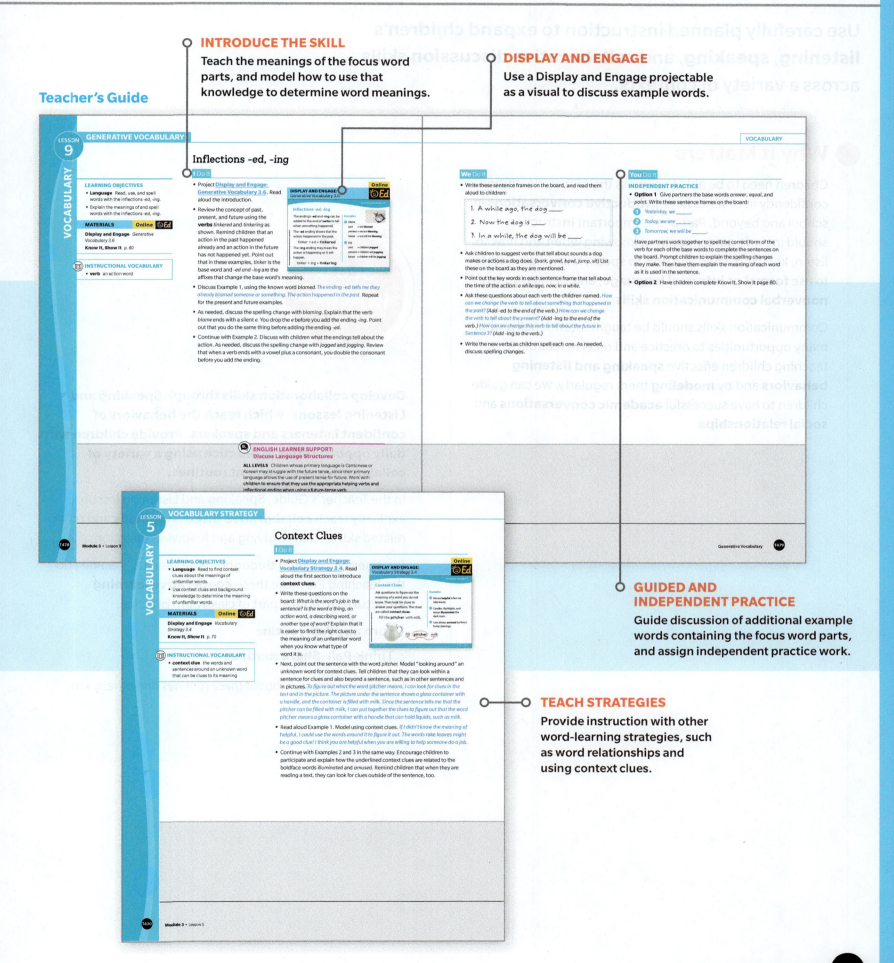

ORAL LANGUAGE AND VOCABULARY
Speaking and Listening

Use carefully planned instruction to **expand children's listening, speaking,** and **collaborative discussion** skills across a variety of contexts.

● Why It Matters

Children need to be able to express their ideas clearly and confidently in order to have **productive conversations** in school and beyond. Part of this important instruction should include guidance about knowing when and how to listen, knowing when and how to speak, knowing whether to use **formal or informal language**, and being aware of **nonverbal communication skills**.

Communication skills should be taught intentionally, with many opportunities to practice and receive feedback. By teaching children effective **speaking and listening behaviors** and by **modeling** them regularly, we can guide children to have successful **academic conversations** and **social relationships**.

See It in Action

Develop collaboration skills through Speaking and Listening lessons, which teach the behaviors of confident listeners and speakers. Provide children with daily opportunities to practice using a variety of collaborative engagement routines.

In the Teacher's Guide, Speaking and Listening lessons explicitly teach **collaborative discussion skills** and other related skills, such as giving and following directions.

Routines highlighted throughout the Teacher's Guide and the Teaching Pal make these **cooperative learning structures** a regular part of classroom practice:

- Turn and Talk routine
- Think-Pair-Share routine

For more information about these routines and others, see pp. 42–43.

TEACHING AND LEARNING

TEACH COLLABORATION SKILLS
Explicitly teach the strategies for successful collaboration and discussion.

ONGOING PRACTICE
Make collaborative discussion and tasks a part of your classroom culture through frequent partner and group tasks.

Teacher's Guide

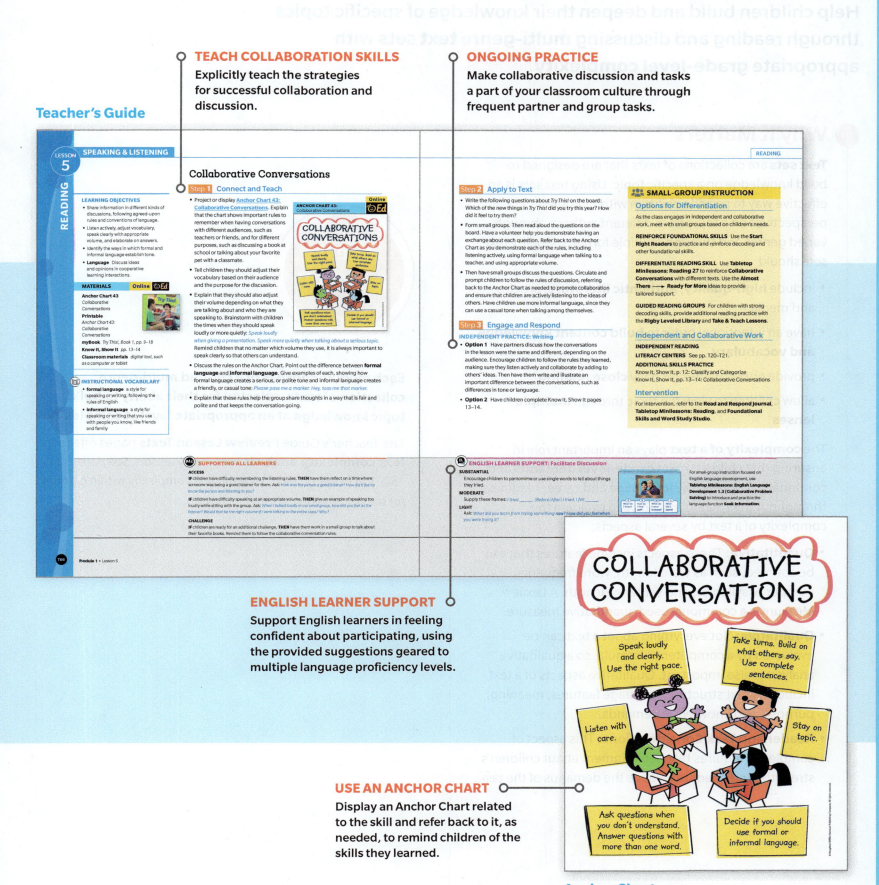

ENGLISH LEARNER SUPPORT
Support English learners in feeling confident about participating, using the provided suggestions geared to multiple language proficiency levels.

USE AN ANCHOR CHART
Display an Anchor Chart related to the skill and refer back to it, as needed, to remind children of the skills they learned.

Anchor Chart

Teaching and Learning 59

READING
Text Sets and Text Complexity

Help children build and deepen their knowledge of specific topics through reading and discussing **multi-genre text sets** with appropriate **grade-level complexity**.

● Why It Matters

Text sets are collections of texts that are designed to build knowledge on a specific topic. Using text sets is an effective way to provide children with multiple perspectives on a topic from different authors, through varied genres and through multiple formats. Quality text sets should

- include **high-quality**, **authentic literature**, articles, and media
- have an intentional order to **build content knowledge and vocabulary**
- provide opportunities for daily **close reading**
- allow children to view the topic through **multiple lenses**

The **complexity of a text** plays an important role in ensuring that children meet **grade-level demands** and continually progress toward college and career readiness throughout their schooling. You can evaluate the complexity of a text by several aspects:

- **Quantitative:** These aspects include features that can be counted, such as word length, word frequency, number of syllables, and sentence length. A Lexile® Measure is a commonly used quantitative measure.
- **Qualitative:** Not everything about a text can be evaluated by a computer or formula, so a qualitative analysis is also important. Qualitative aspects of a text include its text structure, language features, meaning, purpose, and knowledge demands.
- **Reader and Task Considerations:** This aspect of complexity requires teacher judgment about children's strengths and needs, as well as the demands of the task.

See It in Action

Each module consists of a curated multi-genre collection of texts, selected for their ability to build topic knowledge at an appropriate level of complexity.

The Teacher's Guide **Preview Lesson Texts** pages offer a **text complexity analysis** with every lesson. *See pages 152–155 in this guide to view the text complexity within a grade for the whole year.*

TEACHING AND LEARNING

Teacher's Guide

WEEK 3

Preview Lesson Texts

Build understanding of this week's texts so that you can best support children in making connections, understanding key ideas, and becoming lifelong readers.

Drum Dream Girl by Margarita Engle
GENRE Poetry

WHY THIS TEXT?
Poetry is a way for children to explore the use of descriptive language to tell a story. Children will read about a Chinese-African-Cuban young girl who sets out to do something only boys on her island could do.

KEY LEARNING OBJECTIVES
- Identify features of poetry.
- Create mental images to deepen understanding.
- Describe the importance of the setting.

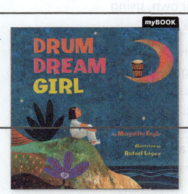

WHY THIS TEXT?
Understand why the text was chosen for the grade and module.

KEY LEARNING OBJECTIVES
Standards-based objectives inform weekly instruction.

TEXT COMPLEXITY

LEXILE MEASURE NP • **GUIDED READING LEVEL** L
OVERALL RATING Very Complex
The text contains some fairly complex, abstract language and a complex story structure.

MAKE CONNECTIONS

BUILD KNOWLEDGE AND LANGUAGE
- **Social Studies Connection:** Important People

VOCABULARY
- **Compound Words:** drumbeats, everyone, drumbeat, outdoor, woodpecker, footsteps, heartbeat, fingertips, outdoors, starlit

FOUNDATIONAL SKILLS
- **High-Frequency Words:** city, looked, heard
- **Vowel Team oo:** boom, moon
- **Multisyllabic Words: oo:** booming, moon-bright, looked, woodpecker, footsteps

SOCIAL & EMOTIONAL LEARNING
- **Self-Management:** Children recognize how a character manages her emotions.

TEXT X-RAY

KEY IDEAS

Key Idea pp. 66–69
A girl dreams of playing the drums.

Key Idea pp. 70–81
Only boys on her island can play drums, so she can only play them in her dreams or in her house.

Key Idea pp. 82–84
The girl's father hires a music teacher to give his daughter lessons.

Key Idea pp. 85–87
After much practice, the teacher says the girl is ready to play the drums at the café. Everyone thinks she plays well and realizes that girls should also be allowed to play the drums.

LANGUAGE

Adjectives
drum dream girl: The author uses two words to describe the main character. As needed, clarify that *drum* and *dream* are frequently used as a noun.

Punctuation
Some English learners may need help understanding that punctuation rules do not apply to poems. In this poem, the author begins each stanza with a capital letter and ends it with a period.

Alliteration
the drum dream girl dreamed (p. 85); *and boom, boom, booming* (p. 87): Tell students that authors use words with the same sounds to add rhythm.

TEXT X-RAY
Preview potential language challenges and cultural references as part of the text's qualitative analysis.

 Module 7 • Week 3

LEXILE MEASURE

GUIDED READING LEVEL

OVERALL TEXT COMPLEXITY RATING
Review the text's overall rating—simple, slightly complex, moderately complex, or very complex—which considers quantitative and qualitative measures.

Teaching and Learning 61

READING
Comprehension Skills and Strategies

Teach children to use skills and strategies to support their **comprehension** and **analysis** of grade-level texts.

🔴 Why It Matters

Reading is not an easy process to master. It must be learned. Some children are able to learn to read and **comprehend** with little or no explicit instruction. They become **skilled readers** on their own, using comprehension strategies automatically.

However, for most children, research has shown that comprehension strategies can be taught—children who have been successfully taught are indistinguishable in their approach to reading from naturally skilled readers. Therefore, most children should receive explicit, systematic instruction in **comprehension skills and strategies** so that they can become effective readers who understand and remember what they have read.

See It in Action

The ultimate goal of reading is to comprehend and build knowledge. Therefore, focus on skills and strategies that will best support the specific text that children are reading. By continually spiraling through skills that are in service of texts, rather than texts being in service of a weekly skill, children will gradually learn to draw from many skills and strategies to comprehend what they read.

Daily Reading lessons in the Teacher's Guide explicitly teach a particular **skill or strategy** before reading, which children immediately **apply** to help them **comprehend** a **read-aloud** or **grade-level text**. The skills repeat often throughout the school year, as children apply them to increasingly complex texts.

Personalized Skills-Based Practice and Support

OPTIONAL CONNECTED RESOURCE

Assign online lessons from *Waggle*® for independent practice to address skills diversity in the classroom.

- Dynamically assesses proficiency and growth in real time
- Supports whole child with SEL-rich content and rewards
- Provides one-click insights to support differentiation
- Available in English

TEACHING AND LEARNING

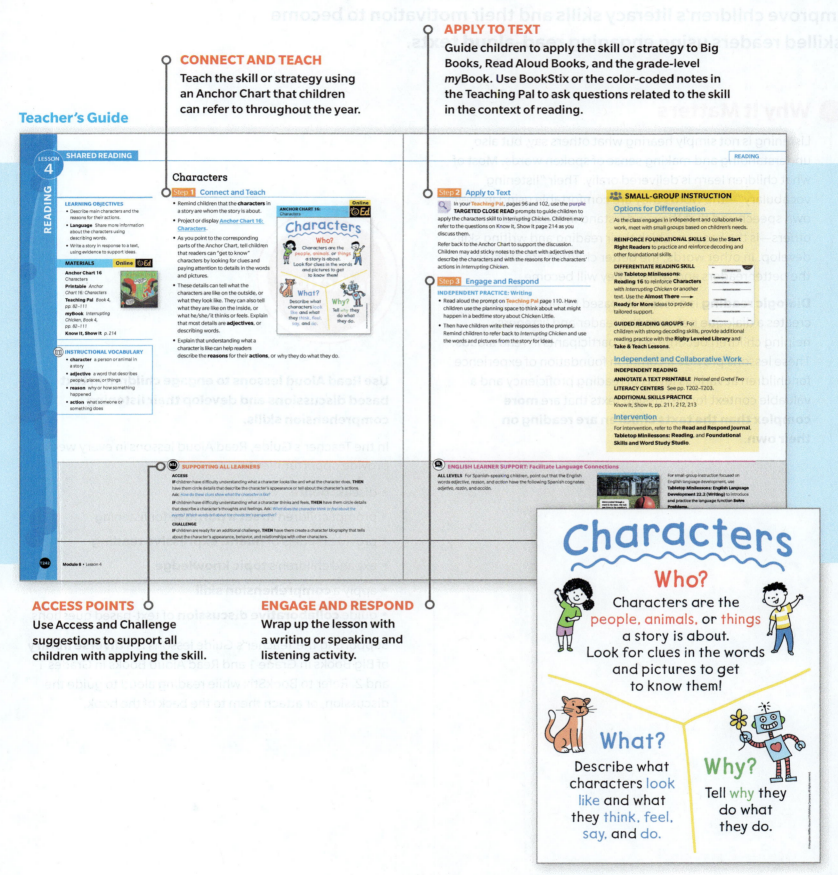

CONNECT AND TEACH
Teach the skill or strategy using an Anchor Chart that children can refer to throughout the year.

APPLY TO TEXT
Guide children to apply the skill or strategy to Big Books, Read Aloud Books, and the grade-level *my*Book. Use BookStix or the color-coded notes in the Teaching Pal to ask questions related to the skill in the context of reading.

Teacher's Guide

ACCESS POINTS
Use Access and Challenge suggestions to support all children with applying the skill.

ENGAGE AND RESPOND
Wrap up the lesson with a writing or speaking and listening activity.

Anchor Chart

Teaching and Learning 63

READING
Dialogic Reading with Read Alouds

Improve children's literacy skills and their motivation to become skilled readers using engaging **read-aloud texts**.

Why It Matters

Listening is not simply hearing what others say, but also understanding and making sense of spoken words. Most of what children learn is delivered orally. Their "listening vocabulary"—the words they are comfortable using in their own speech and that they understand in the speech of others—is the base on which their reading and writing skills develop. In other words, the better children are at listening, the better readers and writers they will become.

Dialogic reading is a research-based technique that creates a dialogue between the reader and listeners, helping children become active participants in read alouds. These lessons provide a common foundation of experience for children at various levels of reading proficiency and a valuable context for discussing texts that are **more complex than the texts children are reading on their own**.

Use Read Aloud lessons to engage children in text-based discussions and develop their listening comprehension skills.

In the Teacher's Guide, Read Aloud lessons in every week provide opportunities to

- discuss **genre**
- prompt children to **set a purpose** for listening
- provide models of **fluent, expressive reading**
- expand children's **topic knowledge**
- apply a **comprehension skill**
- guide **collaborative discussion** of text-based questions

Supporting the Teacher's Guide lessons is a **diverse library** of Big Books in Grade 1 and Read Aloud Books in Grades 1 and 2. Refer to BookStix while reading aloud to guide the discussion, or attach them to the back of the book.

TEACHING AND LEARNING

Teacher's Guide

INTRODUCE THE TEXT
Introduce the genre of the text and have children set a purpose for listening.

MODEL FLUENCY
Read aloud the text to children while modeling the week's fluency skill intentionally.

USE PROMPTS
Use the provided prompts on BookStix to pause occasionally, ask a question about the text, and guide children to apply the skill you introduced in the Teacher's Guide lesson.

ENGAGE CHILDREN
Use the "Children Will Love to …" ideas to focus on the unique features of each book.

BookStix

Read Aloud Book

Teaching and Learning 65

READING
Shared Reading

Teach **comprehension and literary analysis** skills and develop **oral language skills** through shared reading and discussion of *my*Book texts.

Why It Matters

Shared reading is an interactive experience in which teachers model the strategies of proficient readers and children join in the reading as prompted by the teacher. The practice of shared reading

- allows all children, regardless of reading level, to engage with **on-level texts**
- provides children with the tools they need to **develop as readers**, **writers**, **and critical thinkers** as they read a common text together
- provides meaningful opportunities for children to **construct meaning** and revisit a text for different purposes
- builds a **classroom community** where children feel empowered to talk about texts

Utilize a powerful close reading protocol for shared reading and text analysis.

The student *my*Book and the Teaching Pal are companion pieces designed to guide children to construct meaning during **shared reading**. In the Teaching Pal, you will find **color-coded notes** containing discussion prompts, which will help you support children's **critical thinking** and text analysis through **multiple reads** for different purposes.

Notice & Note   Strategies for Close Reading

Develop **active readers** using Notice & Note strategies for close reading, grounded in the research of **Kylene Beers** and **Robert E. Probst**. At the heart of Notice & Note are **Signposts**—significant moments in literary and informational texts that are worth paying attention to. Each Signpost is associated with an **Anchor Question** that helps readers understand and respond to **critical aspects of fiction and nonfiction texts.**

HMH Into Reading seamlessly integrates Notice & Note instruction into the Teaching Pal during shared reading. Look for the **red color-coded notes** like the one on the next page. See pp. 156–159 to preview the Signposts, understand how to introduce the focus Signposts at the beginning of each module, and refer to the fiction and nonfiction texts that feature each Signpost.

Anchor Chart

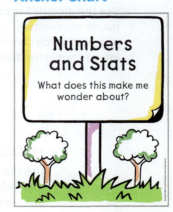

TEACHING AND LEARNING

READ FOR UNDERSTANDING
During a first reading, use the blue questions and prompts to help children get the gist of the text.

Notice & Note
Use the red notes to help children recognize Signposts that alert readers to significant moments in the text and help readers create meaning.

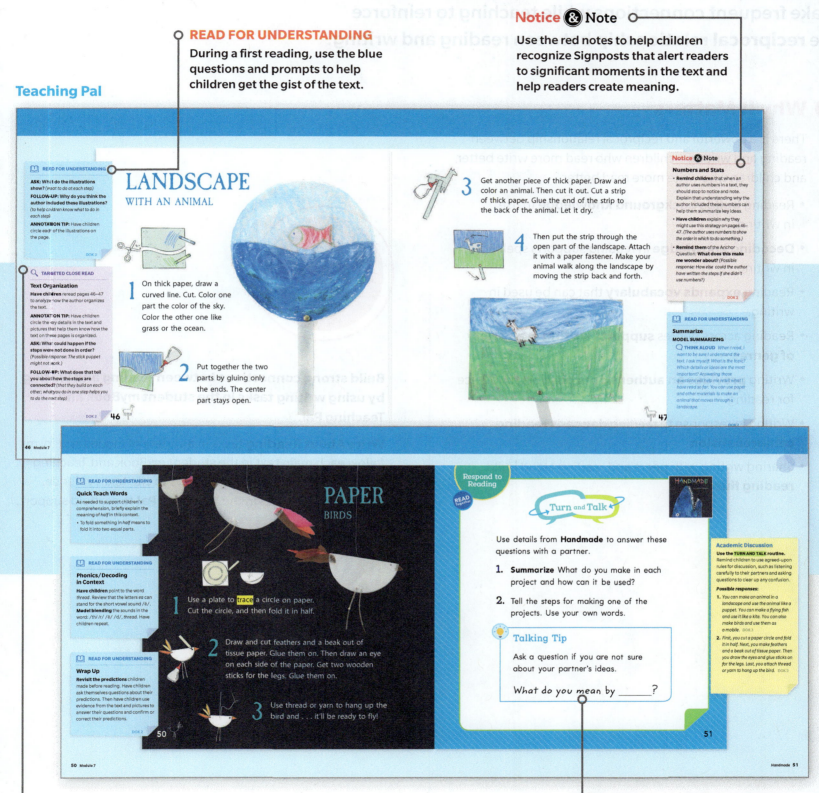

TARGETED CLOSE READ
In subsequent readings, use the purple notes to have children closely analyze sections of the text to apply skills and to gain a deeper understanding of the text.

COLLABORATIVE DISCUSSION
Have children Turn and Talk following each text to practice citing evidence and justifying their reasoning.

READING
Writing in Response to Texts

Make frequent connections while teaching to reinforce the **reciprocal relationship** between reading and writing.

Why It Matters

There is a powerful and reciprocal relationship between reading and writing—children who read more write better, and children who write more read better.

- Reading **builds background knowledge** to use in writing.
- **Decoding knowledge** in reading supports spelling in writing.
- Reading **expands vocabulary** that can be used in writing.
- Reading across genres **supports writing in a variety of genres**.
- Writing **provides an authentic purpose** and audience for reading.
- Writing in response to reading **deepens reading comprehension**.
- Sharing writing with peers and reading aloud build **reading fluency**.

Build strong connections between reading and writing by using writing tasks in the student *my*Book and Teaching Pal.

Write About Reading tasks in a variety of modes and forms follow each main text in the student *my*Book and Teaching Pal, including consistent reminders to cite text evidence. Use the yellow notes in the **Teaching Pal** to scaffold support, as needed.

TEACHING AND LEARNING

Teaching Pal

CITE TEXT EVIDENCE
Remind children to cite evidence from their reading to support a response.

PROMPT
Discuss a prompt that relates to the *myBook* text children just read.

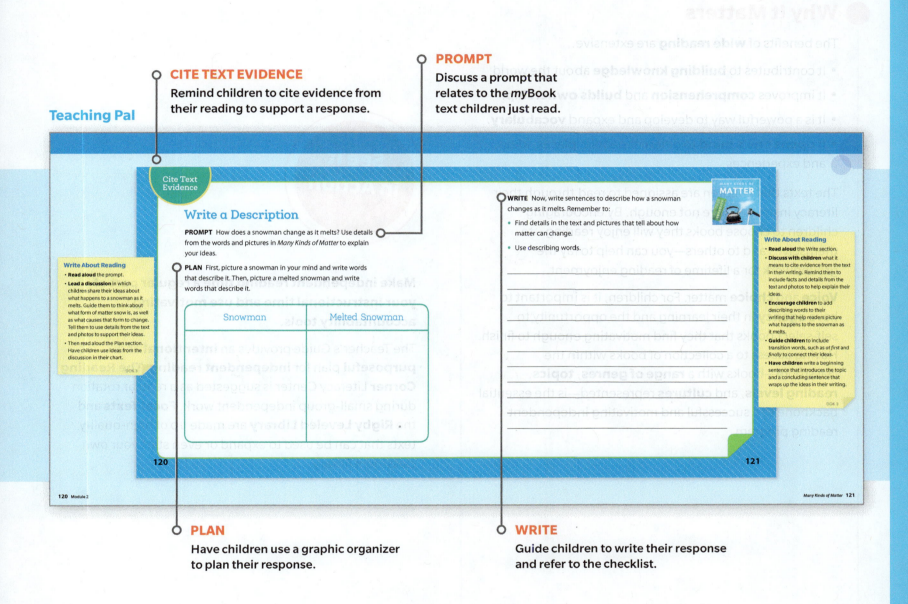

PLAN
Have children use a graphic organizer to plan their response.

WRITE
Guide children to write their response and refer to the checklist.

Teaching and Learning 69

READING
Independent Reading

Give children access to the tools and resources they need to become **independent** and **enthusiastic** readers.

 ## Why It Matters

The benefits of **wide reading** are extensive.

- It contributes to **building knowledge** about the world.
- It improves **comprehension** and **builds ownership**.
- It is a powerful way to develop and expand **vocabulary**.
- It **opens one's mind** to different people, places, ideas, and experiences.

The texts that children are assigned to read through their literacy instruction are not enough. By encouraging children to choose books they will enjoy reading—to themselves and to others—you can help to lay the groundwork for a lifetime of reading enjoyment.

Voice and **choice** matter. For children, it is important to have **agency** in their learning and the opportunity to self-select books that they find motivating enough to finish. Having access to a collection of books within the classroom—books with a **range of genres**, **topics**, **reading levels**, and **cultures** represented—is the essential backbone to a successful and motivating independent reading program.

Make independent reading time a regular part of your instructional time and use motivating accountability tools.

The Teacher's Guide provides an **intentional** and **purposeful** plan for **independent reading**. **The Reading Corner** Literacy Center is suggested as a regular rotation during small-group independent work. **Focal Texts** and the **Rigby Leveled Library** are made up of high-quality texts that can be used to expand or even start your own classroom library.

TEACHING AND LEARNING

Teacher's Guide

SELF-SELECTED READING
Include independent reading time in your regular Literacy Center rotations.

MODULE 2 • WEEK 1

DIGITAL STATION

Listener's Choice
- Have children listen to the Read Aloud Book *The Important Book* or a Leveled Reader of their choice.
- Tell them to add the book to their **Printable: Listening Log**, as well as the active listening skills they used, a summary, and a question they have about the book.

Online Ed

READING CORNER

Independent Reading
- Have children self-select or continue reading an independent reading book.
- Remind children to set a purpose for reading and to record their progress on their **Printable: Reading Log**.
- You may want to choose from these additional options to have children interact with their books:
  » **Read for Fluency** Children use the **PARTNER READING** routine to practice the week's fluency skill, phrasing, or another area of need.
  » **Annotate the Text** Children practice a strategy and use sticky notes to record questions or what they are thinking as they read. Review the sticky notes while you confer with children.
  » **Response Journal** Children draw or write about what they read.

TEAMWORK TIME

Inquiry and Research Project: An Important Book of Matter
- Have groups begin the module project.
- Remind children that their focus this week is to think about and research things that have different properties and post them to the Curiosity Board. *See pp. T192–T193.*

Focal Texts

Rigby LEVELED LIBRARY

Literacy Centers T203

INTERACT WITH BOOKS
Use a variety of options to have children engage with their books and keep independent reading time interesting. Reading logs and response journals are a few of the provided options.

CLASSROOM LIBRARY
Expand your classroom library with these independent reading books, which include a variety of genres, topics, and lengths.

Focal Texts

Grade 1

Grade 2

Teaching and Learning 71

OPTIONS FOR DIFFERENTIATION
Small-Group Instruction

Provide differentiated instruction to children in small groups to **reinforce**, **extend**, and **intervene**.

● Why It Matters

Small-group instruction allows you to tailor instruction to individual children's needs, giving them support with the skills or practice they need to move forward and become skilled readers. Instruction in this context also helps you to **identify gaps** in children's learning, **break down** concepts, and provide **immediate feedback**.

By having a place to closely evaluate what each child is able to do, you can **react** and **support** your students immediately.

See It in Action

Choose from a variety of flexible program resources to provide small groups with targeted support.

Daily options to help you reinforce, extend, or intervene are presented in the Teacher's Guide and supported through a variety of ancillary components.

- In **foundational skills groups**, have children apply new target phonic elements to a decodable Start Right Reader.

- In **skill and strategy groups**, use **Tabletop Minilessons: Reading** to scaffold children's understanding of a skill as they apply it to grade-level text.

- Using **Tabletop Minilessons: English Language Development**, meet with **English learners** to support them at their identified language proficiency level.

- In **guided reading groups**, choose books based on reading level and frequently regroup children based on assessment data.

- To **intervene**, use lessons from the **Foundational Skills and Word Study Studio** or the **Read and Respond Journal**, as appropriate.

For more information about providing differentiated support and intervention, see pp. 100–101.

While you meet with small groups, have other children work on the provided weekly **Literacy Center** activities and daily **independent work options**. *For more information about Literacy Centers, see pp. 114–117.*

TEACHING AND LEARNING

Tabletop Minilessons: Reading

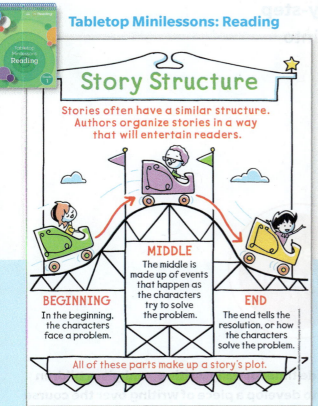

Student-Facing

Teacher-Facing

DIFFERENTIATE READING SKILL
Reteach a reading skill or strategy that children have not yet mastered or connect to the day's whole-class skill to reinforce learning.

SCAFFOLD AND EXTEND
Choose from Almost There → Ready for More options to meet children's individual needs during instruction.

GRAPHIC ORGANIZER
Use a graphic organizer with children to apply the skill to a text.

Tabletop Minilessons: English Language Development

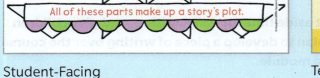

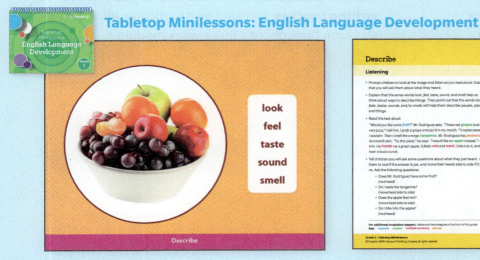

Student-Facing

Teacher-Facing

ENGLISH LEARNER SUPPORT
Introduce or review and practice a language function in the context of the daily reading.

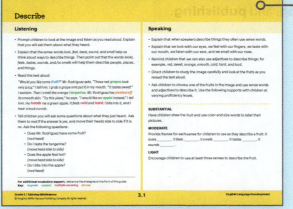

GUIDED READING GROUPS
Select from flexible Take and Teach lessons to use with the Rigby Leveled Library.

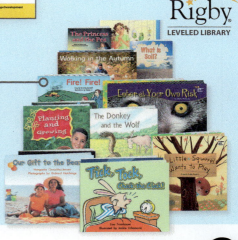

Teaching and Learning 73

WRITING WORKSHOP
Writing Process

When children **learn**, **practice**, and **internalize** a **step-by-step plan for writing**, they become efficient at turning ideas into published writing products.

● Why It Matters

Writing well is an essential aspect of participating in a wide range of school, social, community, and professional activities. People who have not acquired basic writing skills may be at a disadvantage for **educational** and **career opportunities**. By teaching writing as a process, teachers convey the fundamental understanding that **good writing develops over time** and requires careful thought and practice.

Writing instruction should include explicit instruction in different **purposes for writing**, so that children recognize that they should take varied approaches to writing for different audiences. In addition, writing instruction should include **models of good writing** so that children can examine the organization, word choice, and other aspects of the form. Because writing and learning to write are complex, it is important to teach children a growing collection of tools and strategies for the different parts of the writing process: **prewriting**, **drafting**, **revising**, **editing**, and **publishing**.

See It in Action

Set aside time for daily writing, and give children a plan to develop a piece of writing over the course of a module.

The Writing Workshop Teacher's Guide provides **daily explicit instruction** and **modeling** for each stage of the **writing process**, focusing on a particular writing mode and form throughout a three-week module.

TEACHING AND LEARNING

Writing Workshop Teacher's Guide

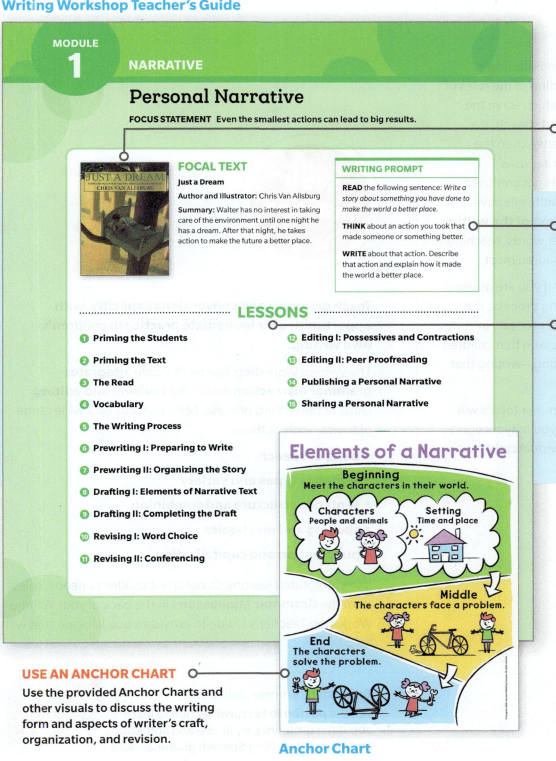

MODULE 1 — NARRATIVE

Personal Narrative

FOCUS STATEMENT Even the smallest actions can lead to big results.

FOCAL TEXT
Just a Dream
Author and Illustrator: Chris Van Allsburg
Summary: Walter has no interest in taking care of the environment until one night he has a dream. After that night, he takes action to make the future a better place.

WRITING PROMPT
READ the following sentence: *Write a story about something you have done to make the world a better place.*
THINK about an action you took that made someone or something better.
WRITE about that action. Describe that action and explain how it made the world a better place.

LESSONS
1. Priming the Students
2. Priming the Text
3. The Read
4. Vocabulary
5. The Writing Process
6. Prewriting I: Preparing to Write
7. Prewriting II: Organizing the Story
8. Drafting I: Elements of Narrative Text
9. Drafting II: Completing the Draft
10. Revising I: Word Choice
11. Revising II: Conferencing
12. Editing I: Possessives and Contractions
13. Editing II: Peer Proofreading
14. Publishing a Personal Narrative
15. Sharing a Personal Narrative

Anchor Chart

MENTOR TEXT
Use an authentic trade book as a mentor text for the module's writing focus.

READ, THINK, WRITE
Introduce and discuss the module's prompt systematically.

WRITING PROCESS
Guide children through the writing process with fifteen lessons, each focused on a different step.

USE AN ANCHOR CHART
Use the provided Anchor Charts and other visuals to discuss the writing form and aspects of writer's craft, organization, and revision.

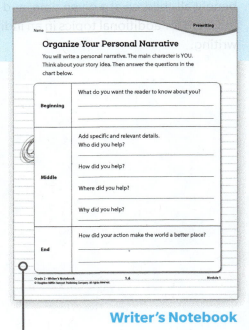

Writer's Notebook

DEVELOP OWNERSHIP
For each prompt, encourage children to record their ideas and thoughts throughout the writing process.

Teaching and Learning 75

WRITING WORKSHOP
Grammar

Provide **integrated grammar instruction** that is meaningful to children's writing.

● Why It Matters

In order to become better writers and communicate effectively, children need an understanding of the rules of **English grammar** and **conventions**, which serve the useful purpose of standardizing print and speech. If a sentence always begins with a capital letter, then the reader is prepared for a new idea. If a writer uses pronouns consistently, then the reader is not confused about who did what. According to research, effective grammar instruction occurs in the **context of the writing process** rather than in isolation. In other words, teaching grammar *through* writing will benefit children most.

What does this look like in a classroom? If you are guiding children through the stages of the writing process, the **revising and editing** steps are the ideal contexts in which to provide a brief grammar minilesson that children can apply immediately to their own writing—writing that they care about.

It is important to be **flexible**. Some grammar topics will benefit all children at a given time, and you may recognize the need for additional topics in an individual child's writing.

Teach grammar and conventions explicitly, with opportunities for immediate practice in children's own writing.

The Writing Workshop Teacher's Guide **integrates grammar instruction** within the **revising and editing** steps of the writing process. Lessons focus on a wide range of topics, such as these:

- **parts of speech**
- **sentence types and variety**
- **sentence structure and combining**
- **spelling and mechanics**
- **punctuation and capitalization**

If the integrated lessons do not meet children's needs, select from the **Grammar Minilessons** in the back of your Writing Workshop Teacher's Guide to provide a quick lesson that will help them.

Spanish Grammar Skills
See the *¡Arriba la Lectura!* section to learn about the program's equitable and authentic approach to teaching Spanish grammar skills.

TEACHING AND LEARNING

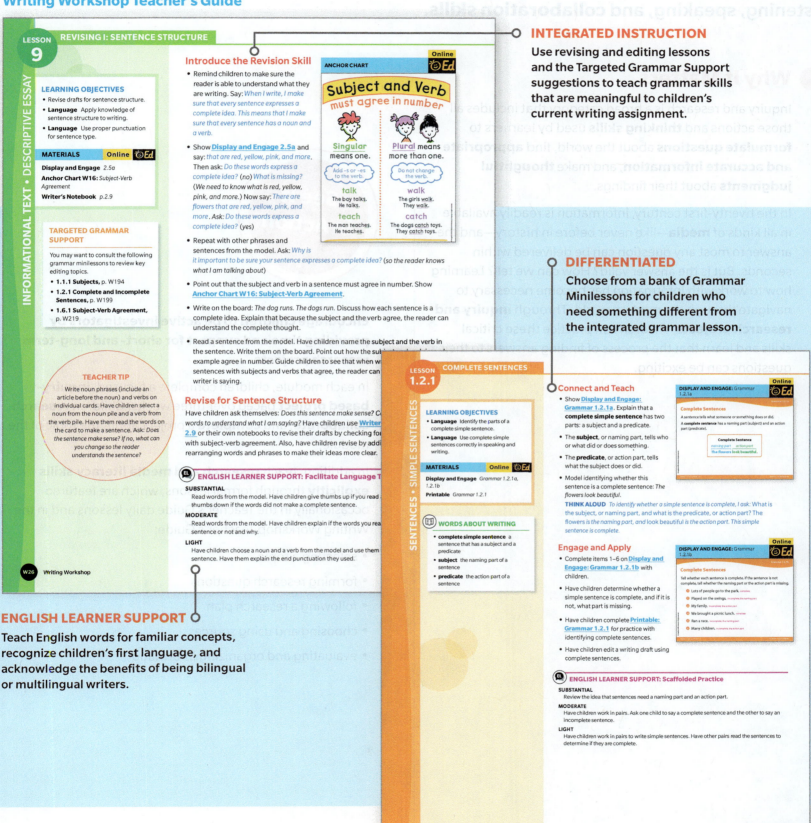

INTEGRATED INSTRUCTION
Use revising and editing lessons and the Targeted Grammar Support suggestions to teach grammar skills that are meaningful to children's current writing assignment.

DIFFERENTIATED
Choose from a bank of Grammar Minilessons for children who need something different from the integrated grammar lesson.

ENGLISH LEARNER SUPPORT
Teach English words for familiar concepts, recognize children's first language, and acknowledge the benefits of being bilingual or multilingual writers.

Teaching and Learning 77

RESEARCH
Inquiry and Research

Engage children in projects that provide opportunities to **extend topic knowledge** while building **research**, writing, listening, speaking, and **collaboration skills**.

● Why It Matters

Inquiry and research is a broad category that includes all those actions and **thinking skills** used by learners to **formulate questions** about the world, find **appropriate and accurate information**, and make **thoughtful judgments** about their findings.

In the twenty-first century, information is readily available in all kinds of **media**—like never before in history—and the answer to most any question can be delivered within seconds. But is the answer valid? How can we tell? Learning how to work with information has become necessary to navigate through the modern world. Through **inquiry and research projects**, children can practice these critical skills and learn that the process of finding answers to their questions can be exciting.

Encourage children to be active investigators by providing time and support for short- and long-term research projects.

In each module, children complete a focused, **inquiry-based project** paced over three weeks. Children **research**, **collaborate**, and **complete** a project about the topic of the module.

In addition, teach **research and media literacy skills explicitly** through formal lessons, which are featured occasionally in the Teacher's Guide daily lessons and in the Writing Workshop Teacher's Guide:

- selecting a topic
- forming research questions
- following a research plan
- choosing and using sources
- evaluating and organizing information

TEACHING AND LEARNING

LAUNCH THE PROJECT
Initiate the brainstorming and research phase, and have children begin research in groups.

TAKE ACTION
Have children develop and execute their project ideas, incorporating visuals, as appropriate.

Teacher's Guide

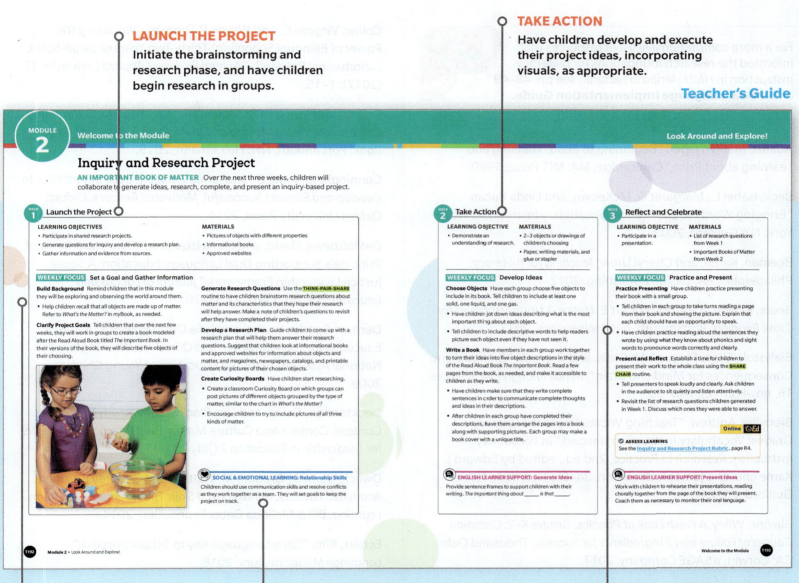

MAKE CONNECTIONS
Connect the project to the module topic, and build background.

RELATIONSHIP SKILLS
Infuse social and emotional learning into every project by reinforcing relationship skills, such as clear communication and negotiating conflicts.

REFLECT AND CELEBRATE
Set aside time for group presentations, and assess children's learning using a project rubric.

Teaching and Learning 79

Research Foundations

Access these professional resources to learn more about the research foundations for *HMH Into Reading*.

For a more comprehensive list of resources that informed the research foundations for biliteracy instruction in *HMH ¡Arriba la Lectura!*, see pp. 48–49 of the **Dual Language Implementation Guide.**

Adams, Marilyn Jager. "Beginning to Read: Thinking and Learning about Print." Cambridge, MA: MIT Press, 1990.

Beck, Isabel L., Margaret G. McKeown, and Linda Kucan. "Bringing Words to Life: Robust Vocabulary Instruction. New York, NY: Guilford, 2002.

Beeman, Karen, and Cheryl Urow. *Teaching for Biliteracy*. Philadelphia, PA: Caslon Publishing, 2012.

Beers, Kylene, & Probst, Robert E. *Notice & Note: Strategies for Close Reading*. Portsmouth, NH: Heinemann, 2013.

Bialystok, Ellen, Fergus I. M. Craik, and Gigi Luk. "Bilingualism: Consequences for Mind and Brain." *Trends in Cognitive Sciences* 16, no. 4 (2012): 240–50.

Biemiller, Andrew. "Teaching Vocabulary In the Primary Grades: Vocabulary Instruction Needed." In *Vocabulary Instruction: Research to Practice*, 2nd ed., edited by Edward J. Kame'enui and James F. Baumann, 34–50. New York, NY: Guilford, 2012.

Blevins, Wiley. *A Fresh Look at Phonics, Grades K–2: Common Causes of Failure and 7 Ingredients for Success*. Thousand Oaks, CA: Corwin, a SAGE Company, 2017.

Blevins, Wiley. *Phonics from A to Z*. 2nd ed. New York: Scholastic, 2006.

Carreker, Suzanne. "Navigating Complex Text: What Students Need to Know and What to Teach." *Lexia Learning*. Accessed November 15, 2018. https://www.lexialearning.com/resources/white-papers/navigating-complex-text-what-students-need-know-and-what-teach.

Collaborative for Academic, Social, and Emotional Learning (CASEL). *The CASEL Guide*. Accessed 2013. http://www.casel.org/guide/.

Collier, Virginia P., and Wayne P. Thomas. "Validating the Power of Bilingual Schooling: Thirty-Two Years of Large-Scale, Longitudinal Research." *Annual Review of Applied Linguistics* 37 (2017): 1–15.

Collins, Kathy, and Matt Glover. *I Am Reading: Nurturing Young Children's Meaning Making and Joyful Engagement with Any Book*. Portsmouth, NH: Heinemann, 2015.

Cunningham, Anne E., and Jamie Zibulsky. *Book Smart: How to Develop and Support Successful, Motivated Readers*. Oxford: Oxford University Press, 2014.

DeMatthews, David, and Elena Izquierdo. "The Importance of Principals Supporting Dual Language Education: A Social Justice Leadership Framework." *Journal of Latinos and Education* 17, no. 1 (2018): 53–70.

Derman-Sparks, Louise, and Julie Olsen Edwards. *Anti-Bias Education for Young Children and Ourselves*. Washington, DC: National Association for the Education of Young Children, 2009.

Dockterman, David, and Lisa Blackwell. "Growth Mindset in Context: Content and Culture Matter Too." *International Center for Leadership in Education* 2 (July 2014).

Dweck, Carol S., Gregory M. Walton, and Geoffrey L. Cohen. *Academic Tenacity: Mindsets and Skills That Promote Long-Term Learning*. Bill & Melinda Gates Foundation, 2014.

Echart, Kim. "Early Language Key to School Success." *Language Magazine*, June 2018.

Echevarria, Jane, Nancy Frey, and Doug Fisher. "What It Takes for English Learners to Succeed." *Educational Leadership* 72, no. 6 (March 2015): 22–26.

Ehri, Linnea C., and Theresa Roberts. "The Roots of Learning to Read and Write: Acquisition of Letters and Phonemic Awareness." In *Handbook of Early Literacy Research*, edited by David K. Dickinson and Susan B. Neuman, Vol. 2, 113–131. New York, NY: Guilford, 2006.

Escamilla, Kathy, Sandra Butvilofsky, and Susan Hopewell. *Biliteracy from the Start: Literacy Squared in Action*. Philadelphia, PA: Caslon Publishing, 2014.

TEACHING AND LEARNING

Foorman, Barbara, Kelley Borradaile, Michael Coyne, Carolyn A. Denton, Joseph Dimino, Lynda Hayes, Laura Justice, Warnick Lewis, and Richard Wagner. *Foundational Skills to Support Reading for Understanding in Kindergarten Through 3rd Grade*. Washington, DC: U.S. Department of Education, Institute of Education Sciences, National Center for Education Evaluation and Regional Assistance. NCEE 2016–4008, 2016.

García, Ofelia, and Li Wei. *Translanguaging: Language, Bilingualism and Education*. Basingstoke, United Kingdom: Palgrave Macmillan UK, 2014.

Genesee, Fred, and Kathryn Lindholm-Leary. "Two Case Studies of Content-Based Language Education." *Journal of Immersion and Content-Based Language Education* 1, no. 1 (2013): 3–33. https://doi: 10.1075/jicb.1.1.02gen.

Graham, Steve, Alisha Bollinger, Carol Booth Olson, Catherine D'Aoust, Charles MacArthur, Deborah McCutchen, and Natalie Olinghouse. *Teaching Elementary School Students to Be Effective Writers: A Practice Guide*. Washington, DC: U.S. Department of Education, Institute of Education Sciences, National Center for Education Evaluation and Regional Assistance. NCEE 2012–4058 June 2012.

Hirsch, E. D., Jr. "Reading Comprehension Requires Knowledge—of Words and the World: Scientific Insights into the Fourth-Grade Slump and Stagnant Reading Comprehension." *American Educator* 27, no. 1 (2003): 10–12, 28–29, 48.

Hougen, Martha C., and Susan M. Smartt. *Fundamentals of Literacy Instruction and Assessment, Pre-K–6*. Baltimore, MD: Brookes Publishing, 2012.

Myers, Diane, Jennifer Freeman, Brandi Simonsen, and George Sugai. "Classroom Management With Exceptional Learners." *TEACHING Exceptional Children* 49, no. 4 (April 17, 2017): 223–30. https://doi:10.1177/0040059916685064.

National Institutes for Child Health and Human Development. Report of the National Reading Panel. Washington, DC: NICHD, 2000.

Neuman, Susan B., and Tanya Wright. "The Magic of Words: Teaching Vocabulary in the Early Childhood Classroom." *American Educator* (Summer 2014): 4–13.

Neuman, Susan B., Tanya Kaefer, and Ashley Pinkham. "Building Background Knowledge." *The Reading Teacher* 68, no. 2 (September 25, 2014): 145–48.

Palmer, Erik. *Teaching the Core Skills of Listening & Speaking*. Alexandria, VA: ASCD, 2014.

Richards, Todd L., Virginia W. Berninger, Pat Stock, Leah Altemeier, Pamela Trivedi, and Kenneth R. Maravilla. "Differences Between Good and Poor Child Writers on fMRI Contrasts for Writing Newly Taught and Highly Practiced Letter Forms." *Reading and Writing* 24, no. 5 (2011): 493–516.

Shanahan, Timothy, Kim Callison, Christine Carriere, Nell K. Duke, P. David Pearson, Christopher Schatschneider, and Joseph Torgesen. "Improving Reading Comprehension in Kindergarten Through 3rd Grade: A Practice Guide" (NCEE 2010-4038). Washington, DC: National Center for Education Evaluation and Regional Assistance, Institute of Education Sciences, U.S. Department of Education. Retrieved from whatworks.ed.gov/publications/practiceguides. 2010.

Templeton, Shane, and Donald R. Bear. "Teaching Spelling in the English/Language Arts Classroom." In *Handbook of Research on Teaching the English Language Arts,* 3rd ed., edited by Diane Lapp and Douglas Fisher, 247–51. New York, NY: Routledge/Taylor & Francis, 2011.

Templeton, Shane, and Donald R. Bear. "Word Study, Research to Practice: Spelling, Phonics, Meaning." In *Handbook of Research on Teaching the English Language Arts,* 4th ed., edited by Diane Lapp and Douglas Fisher, 206–31. New York, NY: Routledge/Taylor & Francis, 2017.

Thiers, Naomi. "Unlocking Families' Potential: A Conversation with Karen L. Mapp." *Educational Leadership: In Sync with Families* 75, no. 1 (September 2017): 40–44.

Thomas, Wayne P., and Virginia P. Collier. *Why Dual Language Schooling*. Albuquerque, NM: Dual Language Education of New Mexico – Fuente Press, 2017.

Wilson, Margaret Berry. "Getting Invested in Routines." *Responsive Classroom*. Accessed December 21, 2015. https://www.responsiveclassroom.org/getting-invested-in-routines/.

Wiseman, Angela. "Interactive Read Alouds: Teachers and Students Constructing Knowledge and Literacy Together." *Early Childhood Education Journal* 38, no. 6 (March 2011): 431–38.

Notes

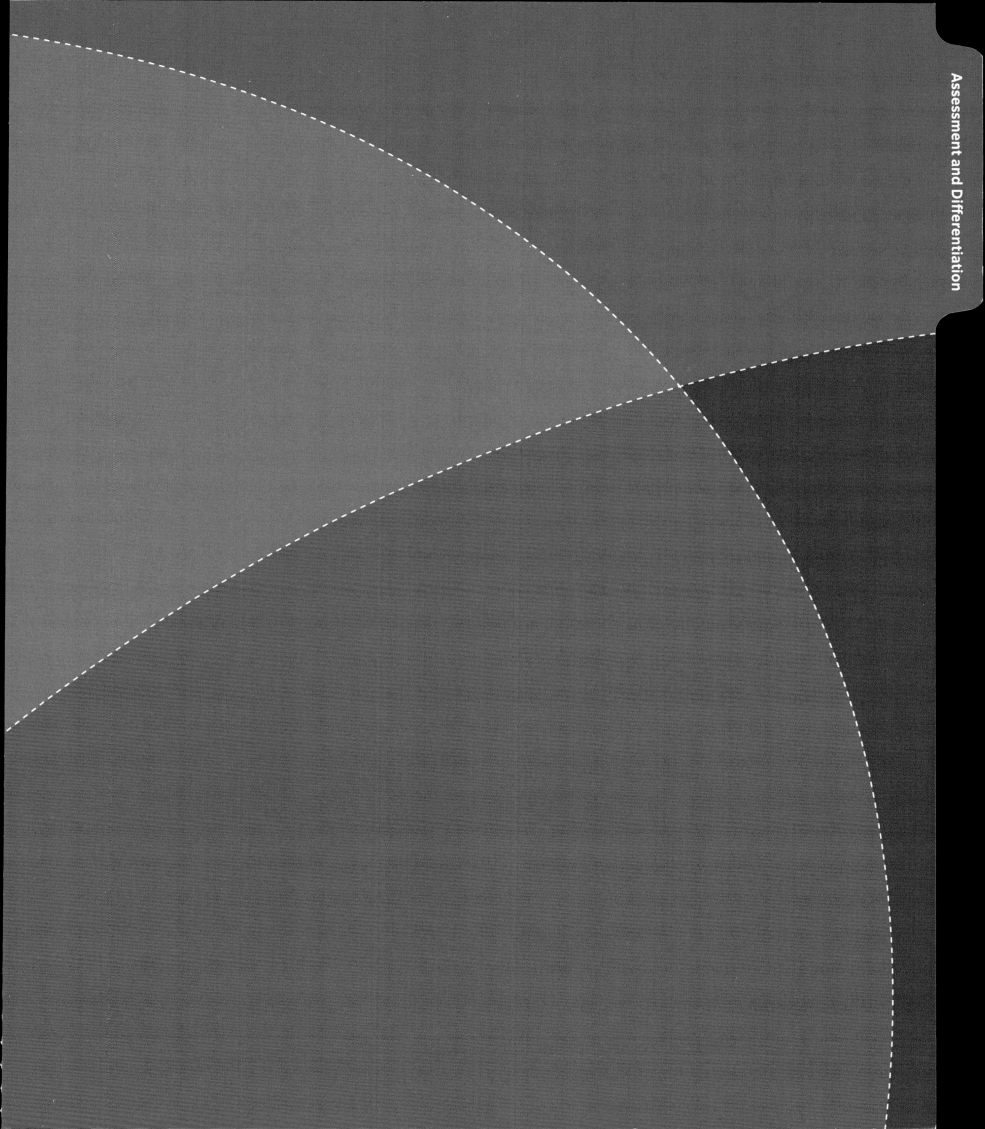
Assessment and Differentiation

Assessment and Differentiation

Data and Reporting	84
Assessments at a Glance	86
Growth Measure	90
Screening, Diagnostic, and Progress-Monitoring Assessments	92
Formative Assessments	94
Assess Writing and Projects	96
Document Students' Growth	98
Provide Differentiated Support and Intervention	100
Support English Learners	102
Meet the Needs of Accelerated Learners	104
Meet the Needs of Special Populations	106
Use Digital Features for Accessibility	108

Assessment and Differentiation

Data and Reporting

Use **meaningful data** that supports timely instruction at each child's level without spending hours on lesson planning.

● Actionable Assessment Data

HMH assessment solutions provide **time-saving tools** to help you **observe**, **measure**, and **understand** where your students are at different points throughout the school year. Reporting connects benchmark assessment data with core in-program assessment data to form a more complete picture of students' proficiency. Assessment data and reporting on *Ed: Your Friend in Learning*® provide actionable insights to target instruction and boost students' growth.

Ed *Ed*, the online learning platform, provides access to all teacher and student program materials, as well as planning, assigning, reporting, and grouping tools. With *Ed*, you can

- **access multiple assessment report views** to see children's gaps and gains at any point throughout the year
- follow children's progress in **standards proficiency** and **access resources** that support mastery
- **look for patterns** in children's errors to choose concepts for reteaching and additional practice
- create and **manage teacher-led small groups**

Standards Proficiency Report

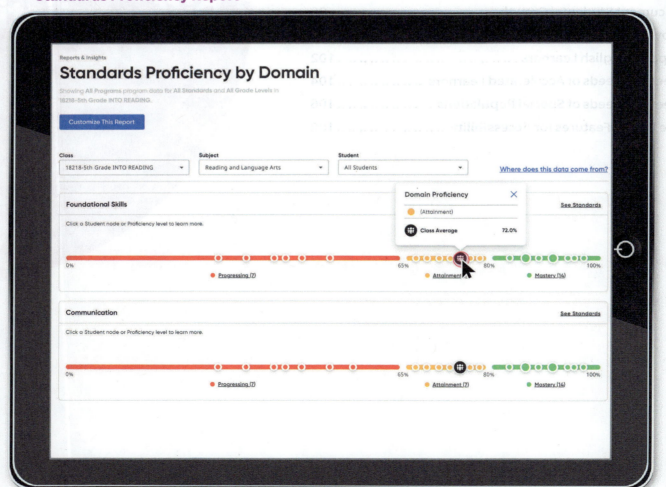

ASSESSMENT AND DIFFERENTIATION

⬤ Customized Grouping

Actionable reports drive **grouping** to facilitate **small-group differentiated instruction**:

- *Ed* **will dynamically group students** based on measurable skill gaps.
- **Customize your groups** or create your own groups.
- **Access tools and resources** that support each group's needs.

Grouping

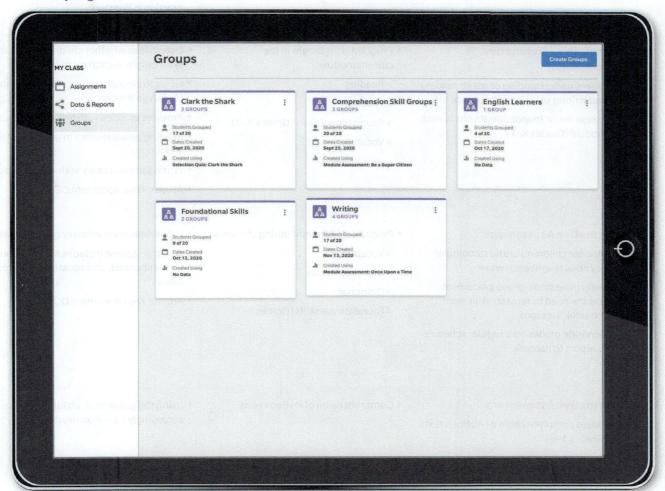

Assessment and Differentiation 85

Assessments at a Glance

Browse the chart for an overview of *HMH Into Reading* and *HMH ¡Arriba la Lectura!* assessments.

Assessment	Purpose	Skills Assessed	Benefits
Growth Measure	**Benchmark Assessment** • Monitor children's comprehension of complex texts (Grades 2–6) • Identify each child's Lexile® range • Measure growth within and across grade levels	• Reading comprehension and language (Grades 2–6)	• Adaptive assessment with automatic scoring provides timely insights into student proficiency • Measures reading comprehension on the Lexile® Framework for Reading • Reports growth at the student, class, grade, school, and district level • Results directly place students into relevant practice in *Waggle®*

Module Assessments	**Formative/Summative Assessment**
	• Assess understanding of major reading and writing skills in each module
	• Assess major foundational skills in each module (Grades K–1)
		• Program skills taught in the current module
		  » Reading
		  » Writing
		  » Foundational skills (Grades K–1)
		  » Vocabulary
			• Determines whether children are mastering skills taught in each module
			• Helps to pinpoint lessons for reteaching or challenge lessons
			• Provides practice with test-taking strategies
			• Reading passages vary in genre, context, and length
			• Writing prompts vary with each assessment
			• Answer Keys document DOK level

Weekly Assessments	**Formative Assessment**
	• Monitor children's understanding of key skills taught each week
	• Determine small-group placement and the need to reteach skills from the week's lessons
	• Generate grades on a regular schedule to report to parents
		• Program skills taught during the week
		  » Vocabulary
		  » Comprehension
		  » Grammar
		  » Foundational skills (Grades K–1)
			• Helps determine mastery of weekly skills
			• Question format includes multiple choice, tech-enhanced, and constructed-response items
			• Answer Keys document DOK level

Selection Quizzes	**Formative Assessment** • Assess comprehension of *myBook* texts (Grades 1–6)	• Comprehension of *myBook* texts	• Using the group tool, children are grouped accordingly based on need
Leveled Readers Running Records	**Formative Assessment** • Record a child's reading behaviors and understanding to provide targeted instruction (Grades K–2)	• Oral reading fluency: provides a passage to read and a place to record errors and self-corrections	• Running records track fluency and support the observation of reading behaviors such as repetition, self-corrections, omissions, substitutions, and insertions • Identifies strengths and weaknesses • Can ask children to do a retelling to get information about sequence and key ideas

FIND OUT MORE on the other pages of this section.

ASSESSMENT AND DIFFERENTIATION

How to Access and Administer	When to Administer/Length
Ed Online Group administered	• Three times a year (fall, winter, and spring) • Nontimed assessment 20–30 minutes
Ed Online or printable PDF Group administered Grades K–1 inventory to individually assess foundational skills in each module is available as a PDF	• At the end of each module • Approximately 20 items per test 30–60 minutes
Ed Online or printable PDF Group administered Can be administered as a whole test or used in sections, depending on need In Kindergarten, comprehension is tested through Listening Comprehension	• At the end of each week • 36 tests • Approximately 10 items per test 15–25 minutes
Ed Online or printable PDF Group administered	• After the first read of each selection • 40 quizzes per grade • 5 items per quiz 5–10 minutes
Ed Printable PDF Individually administered	Varies 10–20 minutes

Assessment and Differentiation 87

Assessments at a Glance

continued

Assessment	Purpose	Skills Assessed	Benefits
Leveled Reader Quizzes	**Formative Assessment** • Understand a child's comprehension of leveled text (Grades 1–6)	• Comprehension of Rigby® Leveled Readers	• Quickly assess general comprehension of a leveled text
Guided Reading Benchmark Assessments	**Formative Assessment** • Determine a child's instructional reading level for guided reading group placement • Identify whether a child is ready to move to the next guided reading level • Assess whether a child is in a guided reading level that is too difficult • Assess at the end of the grading period	• Reading accuracy • Reading comprehension • Retelling	• Each book in the kit contains paired fiction/nonfiction selections • Informs guided reading level small grouping
Screening, Diagnostic, and Progress-Monitoring Assessments	**Screening, Diagnostic, and Progress-Monitoring** • Identify children who start the year with reading difficulties • Determine whether interventions are needed • Learn about a child's specific needs to help target intervention • Monitor progress of children receiving intervention	*Screening* Grades K–1: Letter Identification, Phoneme Segmentation Grade 1: Nonsense-Word Reading Grades 1–2: Word Identification Grade 1 (Mid-Year), Grades 2–6: Oral Reading Fluency *Diagnostic* • Print Concepts Inventory • Letter-Sound Correspondence • Phonological Awareness Inventory *Progress-Monitoring* Grade K: Phonemic Awareness, Letter Naming (Mixed Upper- and Lowercase), Letter-Sound Correspondence Grades K–1: High-Frequency Words, Decoding, Sentence Reading Grades 2–6: Oral Reading Fluency	• Quickly assesses skills related to success of beginning readers and writers • Identifies strengths and needs • Identifies children who need early intervention • Monitors progress after receiving intervention instruction
Amira Learning OPTIONAL CONNECTED RESOURCE	**Formative Assessment** • Oral reading fluency practice and assessment (Grades K–3) • Dyslexia screener (Grades K–3)	*Oral Reading Fluency Assessment* • Oral reading fluency *Dyslexia Screener* • Alphabet knowledge, phonological awareness, word reading	• Powered by AI technology, assesses a child's reading fluency to automatically generate a running record • Dyslexia Screener provides powerful support for early intervention efforts • Provides *HMH Into Reading* content recommendations

FIND OUT MORE on the other pages of this section.

ASSESSMENT AND DIFFERENTIATION

How to Access and Administer	When to Administer/Length
Ed Online or printable PDF Individually administered	After guided reading lesson with a particular reader • 5 items per quiz 5–10 minutes
Located in the Guided Reading Benchmark Assessment Kit **Ed** Online Levels D–W Fiction Comprehension Check and Nonfiction Comprehension Check Individually administered	• One assessment per guided reading level, Levels A–W • 1 reading accuracy check, 1 retelling check, and 10 comprehension items per guided reading level 20–30 minutes
Ed Printable PDF Individually administered	*Screening and Diagnostic* • Beginning of school year • Mid-year in Grades K–1 • Periodically as needed with new children or to assess individual progress • Can select parts to use that are appropriate for your children 30–45 minutes *Progress-Monitoring* Every two weeks 10–20 minutes
Ed Online	Monthly or as needed 7–9 minutes

Assessment and Differentiation

Growth Measure

Use a valid and reliable **research-based assessment** that measures reading skills and **longitudinal progress**.

● Reading Performance and Achievement

How do you know if your students are improving in their reading achievement? Formative assessments, such as observations, questioning, and quizzes, provide immediate feedback to help you modify instruction. While you can gauge your students' progress with formative assessments, a **benchmark assessment**, or reading growth measure, provides you with an actual measurement of reading performance and achievement across the year.

● Performance Data

Beginning in Grade 2, the HMH **Growth Measure** connects the rich standards-based program assessments with a valid and reliable benchmark assessment to provide a more complete picture of a child's knowledge, growth, and skill gaps. Growth Measure is a computer-adaptive test (CAT) that **adjusts item difficulty to children's responses**.

- When a child correctly answers questions, the Lexile® measure of the next question increases.
- If a child answers a question incorrectly, the next question presented is at a lower Lexile® measure.
- The assessment ends once the child has answered enough questions to determine an accurate Lexile® measure.

GROWTH REPORT

Student Growth reports can tell you each child's

- Lexile range
- proficiency in reading comprehension and language domains
- growth across various points in the year

ASSESSMENT AND DIFFERENTIATION

● Assessment Details and Benefits

Ed **Growth Measure** is available online on *Ed: Your Friend in Learning*®:

- Research-based assessment for **comprehension** and **language**
- **Group administered** online three times a year (fall, winter, spring)
- Provides a **snapshot of student reading level and proficiency**
- Helps teachers identify children who are at risk to **drive instructional next steps**
- Automatic scoring reports show growth at the **student, class, and district level**
- **Assign** directly from *Ed*, providing a **consistent user experience** across assessment and core programs

ITEM FEATURES

Assessment items do not require prior knowledge of ideas outside of the passage, do not test on vocabulary out of context, and do not require formal logic.

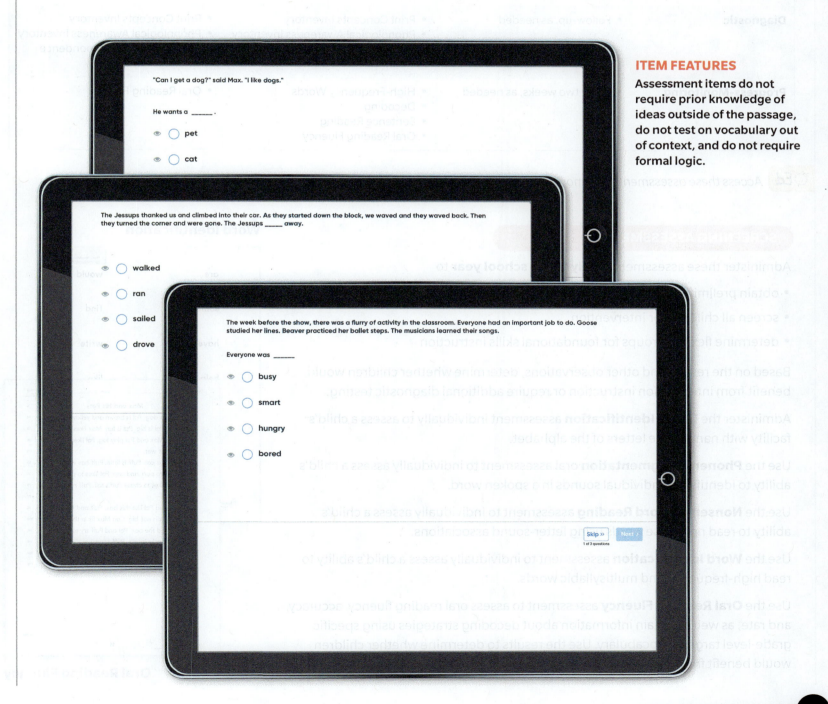

Screening, Diagnostic, and Progress-Monitoring Assessments

Use these assessments to **identify areas for intervention, plan flexible groups** for teaching, and **monitor progress** throughout the year.

Grades 1–2 Assessments

Assessment Type	Frequency	Assessed in Grade 1	Assessed in Grade 2
Screening	• Beginning of year • Mid-year (Grade 1)	• Letter Identification • Phoneme Segmentation • Nonsense-Word Reading • Word Identification • Oral Reading Fluency	• Word Identification • Oral Reading Fluency
Diagnostic	• Follow-up, as needed	• Print Concepts Inventory • Phonological Awareness Inventory • Letter-Sound Correspondence	• Print Concepts Inventory • Phonological Awareness Inventory • Letter-Sound Correspondence
Progress-Monitoring	• Every two weeks, as needed	• High-Frequency Words • Decoding • Sentence Reading • Oral Reading Fluency	• Oral Reading Fluency

Ed *Access these assessments and more information online.*

SCREENING ASSESSMENTS

Administer these assessments **early in the school year** to

- obtain preliminary information about children's performance
- screen all children for intervention
- determine flexible groups for foundational skills instruction

Based on the results and other observations, determine whether children would benefit from intervention instruction or require additional diagnostic testing.

Administer the **Letter Identification** assessment individually to assess a child's facility with naming the letters of the alphabet.

Use the **Phoneme Segmentation** oral assessment to individually assess a child's ability to identify the individual sounds in a spoken word.

Use the **Nonsense-Word Reading** assessment to individually assess a child's ability to read nonsense words using letter-sound associations.

Use the **Word Identification** assessment to individually assess a child's ability to read high-frequency and multisyllabic words.

Use the **Oral Reading Fluency** assessment to assess oral reading fluency, accuracy, and rate, as well as obtain information about decoding strategies using specific grade-level targeted vocabulary. Use the results to determine whether children would benefit from intervention instruction or require additional diagnostic testing.

Word Identification

Oral Reading Fluency

ASSESSMENT AND DIFFERENTIATION

DIAGNOSTIC ASSESSMENTS

Administer the diagnostic assessments as needed to

- follow up with children who score below expectation on the screening assessments
- obtain detailed information to inform skills-based flexible groups and targeted instruction

Use the **Print Concepts Inventory** with children who struggle with letter identification to determine whether they would benefit from instruction in concepts of print. Then re-administer it to monitor progress throughout the year.

Administer the **Phonological Awareness Inventory** to children who struggle with phoneme segmentation to determine whether they would benefit from additional phonological awareness instruction. The skills assessed include words in a sentence; blending, segmenting, and deleting syllables/phonemes; adding/substituting phonemes; rhyme; onset and rime blending and segmentation; and phoneme isolation.

The **Letter-Sound Correspondence** assessment determines a child's ability to associate letters with sounds.

PROGRESS-MONITORING ASSESSMENTS

Administer these three-to-five-minute oral assessments to individuals approximately every two weeks to

- measure growth in reading skills
- identify challenging areas for reteaching, review, and extra practice
- provide checks on children's beginning reading skills
- monitor progress of children who are receiving intervention
- help determine when children are ready to exit intervention

Progress-Monitoring Assessment

Letter-Sound Correspondence

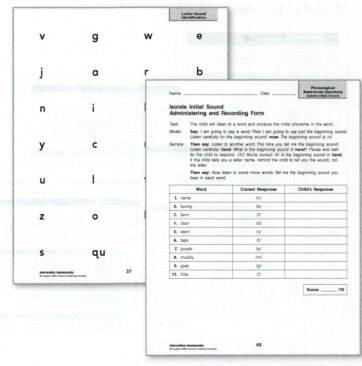

Phonological Awareness Inventory

Assessment and Differentiation 93

Formative Assessments

Use formative assessments to determine **children's mastery** of skills and to plan for **review, reteaching,** or **differentiation.**

● Weekly and Module Assessments

The **Weekly and Module Assessments** measure children's understanding at the end of each week and module.

Each assessment has multiple sections:

- The **Reading** section assesses comprehension and vocabulary skills.
- The **Foundational Skills** section, only in Grade 1, assesses phonics skills and high-frequency words.
- The **Writing** section assesses grammar and writing skills.

Children may take the online assessments flexibly, depending on your access to computers or devices. If you use the paper-and-pencil assessment, administer it as a group and allow as much time as children need to complete it.

 Access guidelines and answer keys for the Weekly and Module Assessments online.

Module Assessment

● Grade 1 Module Inventories

Administer the one-to-one **Module Inventory** to assess foundational skills in more depth as needed. Use some or all parts of the inventory depending on children's needs:

- **Part 1: Phonological Awareness** Orally prompt the child to demonstrate phonological awareness skills, such as producing rhymes and blending phonemes to say words.
- **Part 2: High-Frequency Words** Point to high-frequency words from the module and prompt the child to read each word with automaticity.
- **Part 3: Decoding** Point to nonsense words and prompt the child to decode the words to demonstrate an understanding of target sound-spellings taught in the module.
- **Part 4: Print Concepts** Use a familiar book from the module and prompt the child to demonstrate an understanding of concepts of print taught in the module, such as book parts or directionality.

 Access the Module Inventories, guidelines, and answer keys online.

Module Inventory

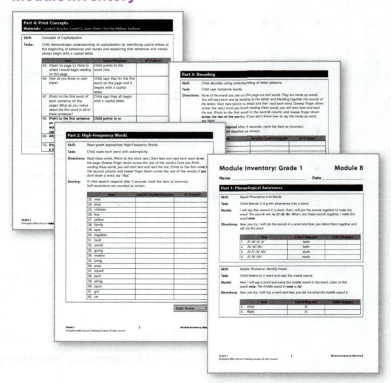

ASSESSMENT AND DIFFERENTIATION

Targeted Skills and Selection Quizzes

Teacher's Guide lessons include embedded opportunities for **formative assessment** of targeted skills during **daily instruction**. Use each lesson's **Independent Practice** and **Engage and Respond** tasks to determine whether children are meeting the learning objectives. Depending on your observations, provide either support or extensions during Small-Group Instruction.

Selection Quizzes are also available to assign after the first read of myBook texts to assess comprehension.

Week 1	Week 2	Week 3	Targeted Skill Practice
Lessons 1–5	Lesson 6–10	Lesson 11–15	Foundational Skills
Lessons 1–5	Lesson 6–10	Lesson 11–15	Reading Skills and Strategies
Lessons 2–5	Lesson 6–10	Lesson 11–15	Vocabulary
Lessons 4–5	Lesson 7–10	Lesson 11–15	Writing and Grammar

Guided Reading Benchmark Assessment Kit

Use the primary **Guided Reading Benchmark Assessment Kit** to determine children's guided reading levels and make instructional decisions.

The kit includes paired fiction and nonfiction selections in each **Benchmark Leveled Reader** for guided reading levels A–N. Including this range of levels allows you to assess accelerated learners in your class beyond the grade-level expectation.

Follow the Teacher Directions in the corresponding **Benchmark Evaluation Guide** for guidance with

- providing an overview of the selection
- assessing oral reading by having the child read aloud while you mark errors
- prompting the child to retell the selection
- assessing the child's comprehension
- using results to determine the child's guided reading level

Every **Leveled Reader** also has a corresponding **Oral Reading Record**.

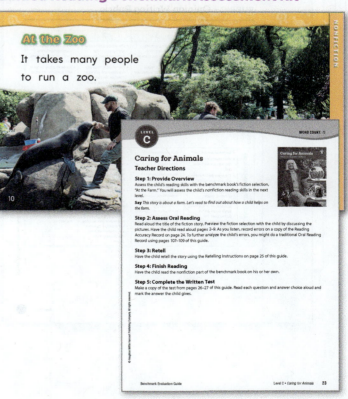

Guided Reading Benchmark Assessment Kit

Assessment and Differentiation 95

Assess Writing and Projects

Use **clear evaluation criteria** to assess children's writing and project work and to provide actionable feedback.

Writing Rubrics

Use rubrics in the Resources section of the Writing Workshop Teacher's Guide or online to assess children's published writing in these areas:

- Organization/Progression
- Development of Ideas/Plot
- Use of Language/Conventions

Writing Workshop Teacher's Guide

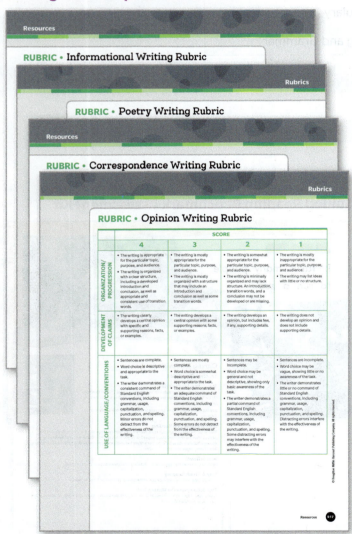

Inquiry and Research Project Rubric

Access the Inquiry and Research Project rubric in the Resources section of the Teacher's Guide, Volume 1, or online to assess children's project work from each module in four key areas:

- Collaboration
- Research and Text Evidence
- Content
- Presentation

Teacher's Guide

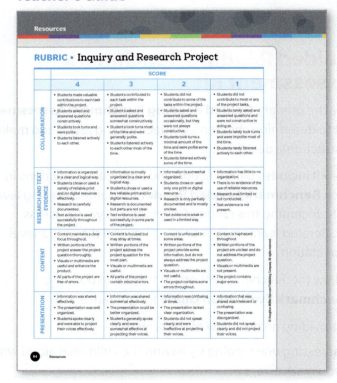

ASSESSMENT AND DIFFERENTIATION

● How to Use the Rubrics

Use specific criteria to **monitor children's growth** in writing types and project work throughout the year. Record notes to clarify scores and reference during conferences.

① Print the rubric from *Ed: Your Friend in Learning*®, or copy it from the Writing Workshop Teacher's Guide or Teacher's Guide. Use a copy for each child.

② Review criteria one at a time as you consider children's work.

③ Record a score for each criterion. Read the descriptors for each score and consider which score best matches the child's performance.

④ Average scores for all of the criteria to determine an overall score of one to four.

Printable Writing Rubric

Informational Writing Rubric II

	SCORE			
	4	**3**	**2**	**1**
ORGANIZATION / PROGRESSION	• The writing is on topic. • The writing is organized with a clear structure and includes an introduction and a body.	• The writing is mostly on topic. • The writing is organized with some structure and may be missing a clear introduction.	• The writing is minimally on topic. • The writing is minimally organized and is missing an introduction.	• The writing is not on topic. • The writing may list ideas with little or no structure.
DEVELOPMENT OF IDEAS	• The writing clearly develops a central idea with specific and relevant details.	• The writing develops a central idea with some relevant details.	• The writing develops an idea, but includes few, if any, details.	• The writing does not develop an idea and does not include details.
USE OF LANGUAGE / CONVENTIONS	• Sentences are complete. • Word choice is specific. • The writer demonstrates a command of conventions most of the time, including capitalization for the beginning of sentences and pronoun "I" and punctuation at the end of sentences.	• Sentences are mostly complete. • Word choice is mostly specific. • The writer demonstrates a command of conventions some of the time, including capitalization for the beginning of sentences and pronoun "I" and punctuation at the end of sentences.	• Sentences may be incomplete. • Word choice includes few specific words. • The writer infrequently demonstrates a command of conventions, including capitalization for the beginning of sentences and pronoun "I" and punctuation at the end of sentences.	• Sentences are incomplete. • Word choice is vague. • The writer rarely demonstrates a command of conventions, including capitalization for the beginning of sentences and pronoun "I" and punctuation at the end of sentences.

Because children at this age are emergent writers, discuss children's responses with them to gain insight into their understanding of the task.

Grade 1 • Rubric
© Houghton Mifflin Harcourt Publishing Company. All rights reserved.

Printable

Assessment and Differentiation 97

Document Students' Growth

Use **informal assessment tools** to gather data and gain a complete picture of children's growth and instructional needs.

⬤ Portfolios

At the beginning of the year, **set up portfolios** for all the children in your class. Consider including the following **formal and informal assessments** in your children's portfolios:

- Screening, Diagnostic, and Progress-Monitoring Assessments (see pp. 92–93)
- Weekly Assessments, Module Assessments, and Grade 1 Module Inventories (see p. 94)
- Oral Reading Records (see p. 95)
- Writing and Project Rubrics (see pp. 96–97)
- Reading Logs (see p. 99)
- Observation Notes (see p. 99)

Collaborate with children to select **work samples** from their portfolios that showcase their best work and document progress throughout the year. Consider the following student work:

- copies of *my*Book work, such as response writing
- completed Reading or Language Graphic Organizers
- handwriting samples from the beginning, middle, and end of the year
- samples of different writing types over the course of the year
- photos of children's inquiry and research projects or other collaborative work

*my*Book Response Writing

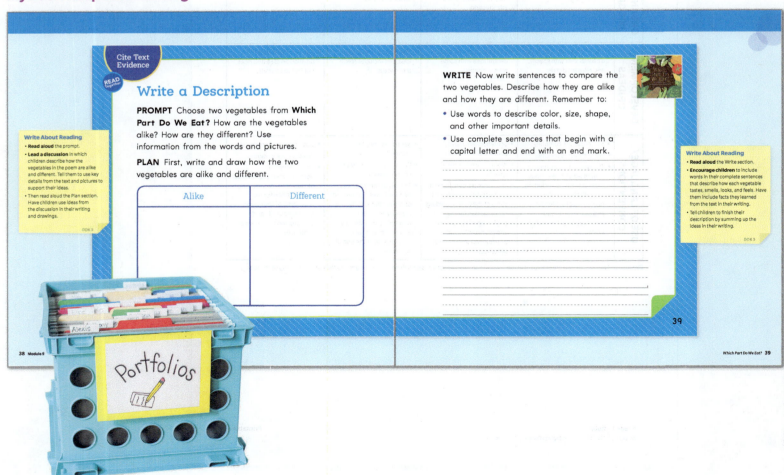

Program Guide • Grades 1–2

ASSESSMENT AND DIFFERENTIATION

● Reading Surveys and Logs

Survey children and their families at the beginning and middle of the year to gather information about their reading interests, attitudes, and preferences. Use the information from surveys to

- recommend books or literacy routines to families
- inform instructional planning
- support children with self-selected reading

Have children complete a Reading Log for their independent reading. Use it to monitor children's reading frequency and what they record about their reading.

Reading Log Printable

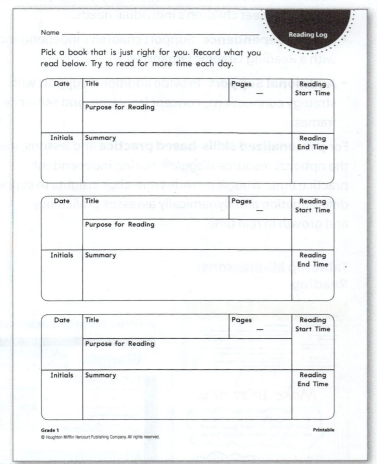

● Observation Notes

Observe children closely and **take notes** during individual conferences, guided reading groups, small-group instruction, and independent reading and writing.

Set up a system for recording and organizing **observation notes** that works for you, and transfer the notes to your children's portfolios. You may consider observing and noting

- reading behaviors children show during guided reading, such as pointing to words, rereading, or self-correcting
- writing strategies children use independently, such as adding details, applying grammar skills, or spelling known or unknown words
- foundational skills understandings children demonstrate during small-group instruction
- examples of children displaying social and emotional competencies, such as Responsible Decision-Making, Social Awareness, Self-Awareness, Self-Management, or Relationship Skills

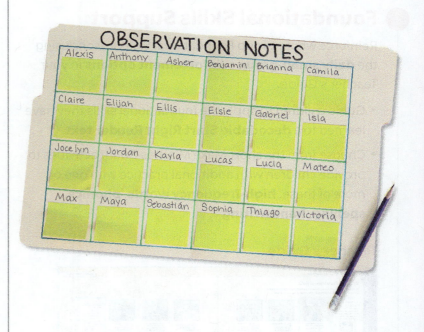

Assessment and Differentiation 99

Provide Differentiated Support and Intervention

Choose flexible resources based on each child's assessed needs to provide the appropriate level of support.

● Embedded Support

In whole-group Reading lessons, use **Supporting All Learners** notes to scaffold instruction.

- Select from **Access** and **Challenge** options.
- Refer to clear **IF/THEN statements** to implement targeted support right in the moment of instruction and practice.

Teacher's Guide

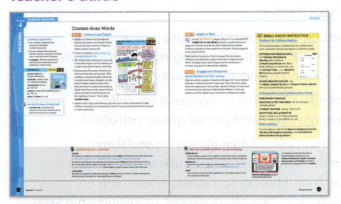

● Foundational Skills Support

Reinforce whole-group Foundational Skills lessons using the **daily small-group reinforcement options** in your Teacher's Guide.

- Guide children to apply the foundational skills they have learned to a **decodable Start Right Reader text**.
- Choose from the short Make Minutes Count activities to provide children with additional practice with one or more of these: **high-frequency words**, **phonics**, **spelling**, **handwriting**.

Teacher's Guide

● Skill and Strategy Support

In small groups, use Tabletop Minilessons: Reading to reteach a skill or strategy that children have not yet mastered or to connect to the day's whole-class skill with scaffolded support to reinforce learning.

- **Anchor the Concept** Use the visual on the front of the flip chart to emphasize key points.
- **Apply to Text** Support application of the concept to the day's whole-class text, an appropriate Rigby® Leveled Reader, or another appropriate text of your choice.
- **Scaffold** Choose from Almost There ⟶ Ready for More options to meet children's individual needs.
- **Build Independence** Support children's independence with a Reading Graphic Organizer.
- **Additional Support** Provide additional support with strategy connections, concept language, and sentence frames.

For **personalized skills-based practice** and lessons, use the optional resource *Waggle®* during independent practice time. *Waggle* provides one-click insights to support differentiation and dynamically assesses proficiency and growth in real time.

Tabletop Minilessons: Reading

OPTIONAL CONNECTED RESOURCE

100 Program Guide • Grades 1–2

ASSESSMENT AND DIFFERENTIATION

Guided Reading Groups

Choose Leveled Readers that match children's instructional levels and target specific reading behaviors in small groups.

- **Assess** Use the Guided Reading Benchmark Assessment to determine each child's instructional level for guided reading groups.
- **Choose Books** Select from the Rigby® Leveled Library, which includes books across a wide range of guided reading levels, genres, and topics.
- **Select Teaching Sessions** Choose flexible teaching sessions from the Take and Teach Lessons to deliver scaffolded instruction.

Take and Teach Lessons

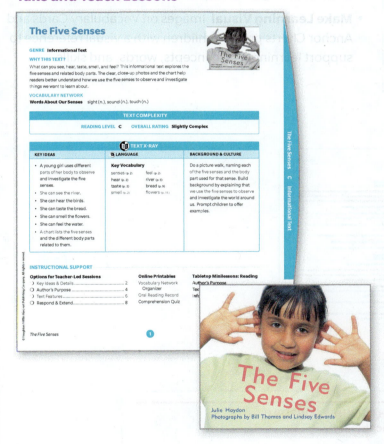

Intervention and Foundational Skills Support

Use the online **Foundational Skills and Word Study Studio** to teach prerequisite foundational skills or reinforce daily foundational skills.

- **Assess** Use screening, diagnostic, and progress-monitoring assessments to determine which foundational skills children need to learn or review.
- **Intervene** Select the appropriate lessons to use during small-group or one-to-one time.

Use the print or online **Read and Respond Journal**, which includes passages written below grade-level, to provide Tier II intervention and help children build confidence as readers.

- **Assess** Determine children's specific needs with data from Growth Measure, Weekly or Module Assessments, observation, and anecdotal notes.
- **Intervene** Assign skill support individually or in small groups and work through the Read and Respond Journal passage together.

Foundational Skills and Word Study Studio

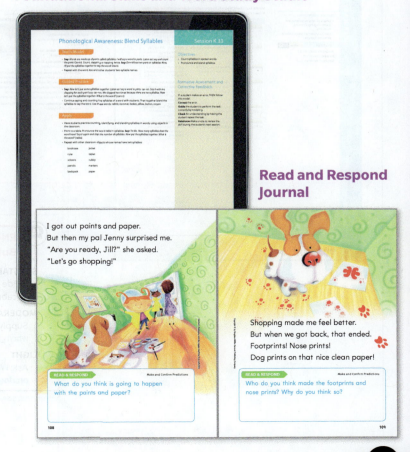

Read and Respond Journal

Assessment and Differentiation **101**

Support English Learners

Provide **targeted language support** to English learners at various levels of proficiency.

● Embedded Support

Use Teacher's Guide lessons with **embedded English Learner Support**—Substantial, Moderate, and Light—for **multiple language proficiency levels** across instructional contexts.

- Look for the **recurring English Learner Support feature** across the bottom section of your Teacher's Guide lessons.
- **Preview the strategies** before teaching a lesson.
- Select the **level of support and the strategy** that best target the needs of the English learners in your class.

In addition to features labeled for English learners, *HMH Into Reading* also embeds **evidence-based strategies** and practices that contribute to all children's learning while also accelerating English learning.

These strategies and practices include:

- **Engage Students** Use engagement routines highlighted throughout the Teacher's Guide lessons to provide frequent opportunities for English learners at all stages of language acquisition to respond verbally in a low-risk group setting.
- **Build Knowledge** Teacher's Guide lessons and Get Curious Videos activate and build children's background knowledge about module topics to support their understanding of concepts, vocabulary, and the texts.
- **Make Learning Visual** Images on Vocabulary Cards and Anchor Charts provide children with a visual reference to support learning new concepts, words, and skills.

Teacher's Guide

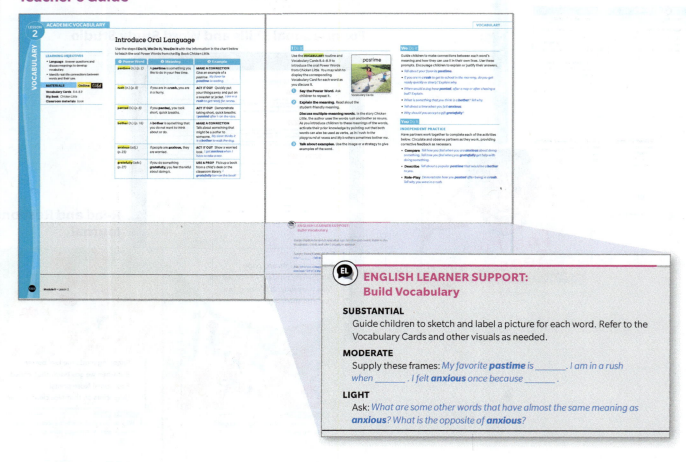

102 Program Guide • Grades 1–2

ASSESSMENT AND DIFFERENTIATION

Small-Group Support

Use Tabletop Minilessons: English Language Development with children in small groups. If most children in your class are English learners and the level of support they need varies, you may decide to form multiple small groups. If you have six or fewer English learners, you may wish to form one group but provide different levels of support.

- **Display images** to spark children's interest and support background knowledge.
- **Deliver daily instruction** at children's **language proficiency level**, using the prompts provided. Each week's instruction focuses on a particular language function across one of these literacy domains: listening, speaking, reading, writing, collaborative problem-solving.
- **Use language supports** such as sentence frames and phrase banks to guide effective expression and empower children's language development.
- **Distribute and discuss** Language Graphic Organizer printables to support use of academic language functions.

Tabletop Minilessons: English Language Development

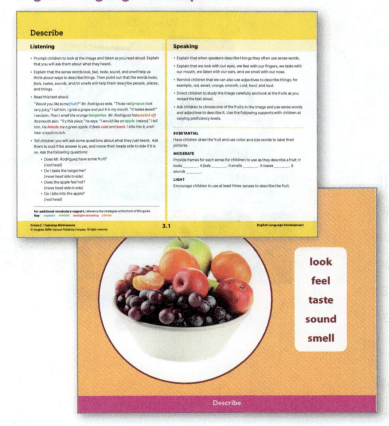

Build Cross-Linguistic Connections

Use the Language Differences online resource to build cross-linguistic connections between English and children's first languages. This resource can help you

- **target specific areas** that are challenging
- identify areas in which children can **leverage knowledge** from their first languages
- become familiar with ways that each language **aligns with or differs from English** in the following areas:
  » **Alphabet** (Writing System)
  » **Phonological Features** (Consonant and Vowel Sounds)
  » **Grammatical Features** (Parts of Speech, Verb Tenses, Sentence Structure, and Syntax)

There are also resources available online to support English learners with articulating challenging sounds. Model the mouth positions for making various sounds using **Articulation Videos**, and access **Articulation Support** printables for model language you can use to describe the mouth positions to children.

Language Differences

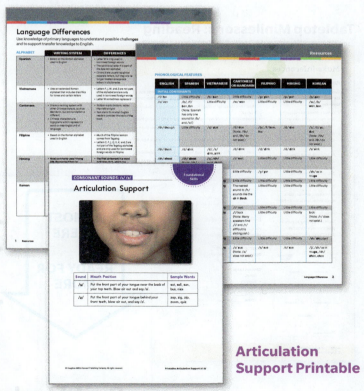

Articulation Support Printable

Ed *Access these resources online.*

Assessment and Differentiation

Meet the Needs of Accelerated Learners

Provide targeted support to children who **exceed grade-level expectations** to keep them engaged and thriving.

● Ready for More

Daily options for differentiation provide support for accelerated learners who are ready for more.

- Teaching support labeled **Supporting All Learners** extends skill and strategy work during whole-group Reading lessons and provides daily opportunities for those children who need a challenge.
- **Rigby® Leveled Library** with **Take and Teach Lessons** may be used to support Guided Reading groups.
- **Tabletop Minilessons: Reading** provide support and Ready for More scaffolds as children apply comprehension skills to higher-level texts they are reading independently.
- **Differentiated Spelling Instruction: Placement Support and Differentiated Lists** is an online resource that can be used to determine children's stage of spelling development and to access spelling lists appropriate to their level.
- **Inquiry and Research Projects** and **Reading Remake Printable** activities in every module provide opportunities for enrichment.
- **Focal Texts** include a variety of challenging books for independent reading.

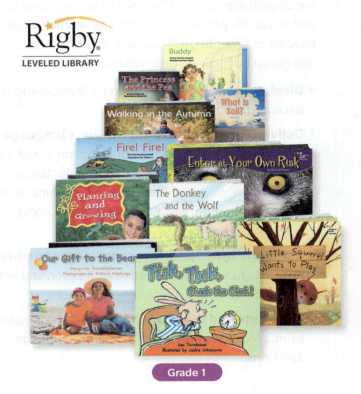

Grade 1

Tabletop Minilessons: Reading

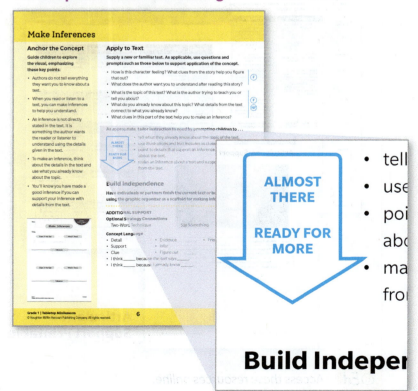

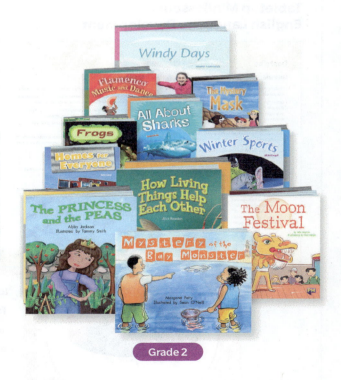

Grade 2

104 Program Guide • Grades 1–2

ASSESSMENT AND DIFFERENTIATION

🔸 Best Practices for Accelerated Learners

Remember these best practices when working with accelerated learners:

- Ensure that **children's "advanced" beginning literacy skills** continue to progress.

- **Use flexible grouping** and avoid forming fixed groups for extended periods of time. Children may be above level for particular skills but not for others, or they may be above level at one point in the year but not remain so.

- Provide opportunities for children to **make their own decisions** whenever possible. Think of ways for accelerated learners to take on leadership roles and assist classmates, when appropriate.

- Keep a **range of texts** in your classroom library that mirror the range of children's reading abilities.

- **Provide alternate, more challenging versions** of activities to engage accelerated learners and go beyond simply assigning more work.

- **Differentiate for accelerated learners** in both small-group and whole-class settings to boost engagement and limit behavioral challenges.

Focal Texts

Grade 1

Grade 2

Assessment and Differentiation 105

Meet the Needs of Special Populations

Build an understanding of the **unique challenges** some children face to help you make decisions about how best to support their learning.

● Challenge: Concept Knowledge and Oral Language

Instructional Focus	Program Supports
Build background knowledge about concepts and content-area topics.	**Get Curious Videos**, **Knowledge Maps**, and lessons support children in building knowledge networks.
Conduct interactive **read alouds** and shared reading to involve children in high-quality discussions about texts.	Interactive read-aloud lessons and **BookStix** include **dialogic reading prompts** for discussion.
Directly teach **academic vocabulary** related to a topic or theme.	A **Vocabulary routine** and lessons using **Vocabulary Cards** provide consistent steps to teach and practice using topic and academic words.
Encourage children to **interact and play with words**.	Generative vocabulary and vocabulary strategy lessons help build **word knowledge.**
Provide scaffolds, such as **sentence frames,** to facilitate children's participation in class discussions.	Lessons include **sentence frames** to support children in structuring **oral and written responses**.
Honor and validate children's **home languages**, and explicitly teach and model the language of school.	**Social communication** and **collaborative discussion lessons** explicitly teach and guide practice of speaking and listening skills.

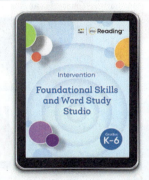

● Challenge: Dyslexia and Word-Reading Skills

Instructional Focus	Program Supports
Provide daily, engaging instruction in **phonological awareness** and phoneme blending and segmenting.	**Daily foundational skills lessons** build phonological awareness skills, including blending and segmenting phonemes.
Support children with **mouth positions** and practice with **articulating sounds**.	**Articulation Videos** and online **Articulation Support** printables provide models and guidance for pronouncing particular sounds.
Directly build automatic recognition of **high-frequency words**.	A consistent **High-Frequency Words** routine reinforces word learning.
Practice new skills and review previously learned ones through **daily reading of connected texts**.	Decodable **Start Right Reader** texts provide practice with reading high-frequency words and words with target sound-spellings in context.
Include daily opportunities for small-group instruction and practice to differentiate instruction for the **range of children's needs** in the class.	**Small-group instruction** gives teachers options for teaching and practicing foundational skills with small groups. **Foundational Skills and Word Study Studio** provides opportunities for strategic intervention in phonemic awareness and phonics.

> **FIND OUT MORE** See **pages 108–109** for more information about accessibility features available online.

ASSESSMENT AND DIFFERENTIATION

● Challenge: Visual, Hearing, Physical, or Cognitive Disabilities

Instructional Focus	Program Supports
• Provide multiple options for children to **understand**, **participate**, **respond**, and **express** themselves.	• The instructional model includes **whole-class lessons**, **small-group instruction**, and options for **building independence**.
• Allow for **variations** in the pace of lessons and in the length of time spent on a given skill or concept.	• Daily lessons are organized so teachers can adjust **pacing and schedules** as needed.
• **Establish routines** and **set goals** to support children as they build executive function skills.	• **Consistent routines** and procedures across lessons help children know what to expect. Resources allow children to set and monitor reading and writing goals.
• Vary the options for expressing **understanding** and **ideas**: verbal and nonverbal, visual and nonvisual.	• **Engagement** and **classroom management routines** provide a variety of options for expression.
• Limit the amount of **sensory stimulation** in the classroom.	• Suggestions for setting up the classroom include minimizing artificial light and **unnecessary visual stimulation** on walls.
• When available and appropriate, provide children with **Braille formats** and supports using **American Sign Language**.	• HMH supports the mission of the **NIMAC**, which distributes NIMAS-conformant files for core student print materials to state and local education agencies to facilitate the creation of large-print, Braille, or other accessible formats.
• Provide features to make content, including videos and eBook texts, **accessible** to children with disabilities.	• The digital content on *Ed: Your Friend in Learning*® includes **WCAG 2.0 AA compliance features**, such as closed captioning for videos, contrast and color compliance, responsive and reflowable design, and pedagogically equivalent text alternatives.

Assessment and Differentiation 107

Use Digital Features for Accessibility

Use digital features to **provide accessibility** for children who have impairments to vision, hearing, cognition, or mobility.

Content Accessibility

Web Content Accessibility Guidelines (WCAG) provide recommendations for making digital tools and technologies accessible for people with disabilities. *Ed: Your Friend in Learning*® follows WCAG 2.0 AA recommendations to meet the needs of diverse learners.

Accessibility Feature	Impairment			
	Visual	Hearing	Cognitive	Mobility
closed captioning for videos		•	•	
transcripts for audio		•	•	
contrast and color compliance	•			
screen reader compatibility (keyboard operability) for platform and content	•		•	•
keyboard encoding for compatibility with many assistive technologies	•	•	•	•
responsive, reflowable design	•	•	•	•
pedagogically equivalent alternative resources	•	•	•	•

Inclusive Design and Innovation

Keep all children engaged with built-in digital features to maintain inclusive learning.

- read-along audio with synchronized text highlighting
- student highlighting and note-taking tools
- point-of-use glossary entries
- pedagogical grade- and level-appropriate text alternatives

ASSESSMENT AND DIFFERENTIATION

• Text Alternatives

When texts include images as part of the learning experience, *HMH Into Reading* and *HMH ¡Arriba la Lectura!* use concise text alternatives that strive to convey the same instructional relevance and engagement to those using assistive technologies, such as screen readers. These thoughtful, pedagogically sound, and engaging text alternatives provide equity in learning for all children.

INFORMATIONAL TEXTS

Informational texts include text alternatives for diagrams, maps, portraits, or other images.

Here is a Grade 4 *myBook* example:

A historic map that shows the plan for the town and harbor of St. Augustine. The Castillo de San Marcos and Fort Mose are pointed out with labels.

LITERATURE

Text alternatives go beyond the basics to create equity in engagement as well. Story illustrations have text alternatives that share important details to create the same engagement for children using screen readers as their peers enjoy.

Here is a Grade 1 *myBook* example:

Brontorina, who is a dinosaur, stands at the entrance of a building. Madame Lucille, the teacher, looks out from the door at the dinosaur. Children are behind her wearing ballet clothing.

Grade 4 *myBook*

Grade 1 *myBook*

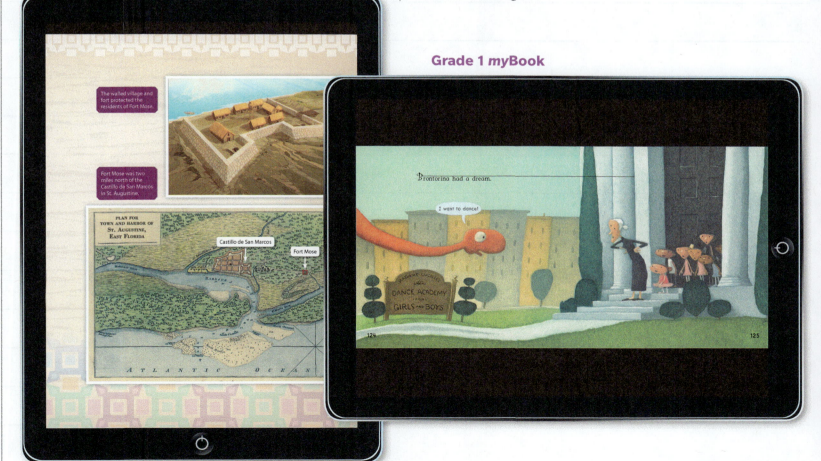

Assessment and Differentiation 109

Notes

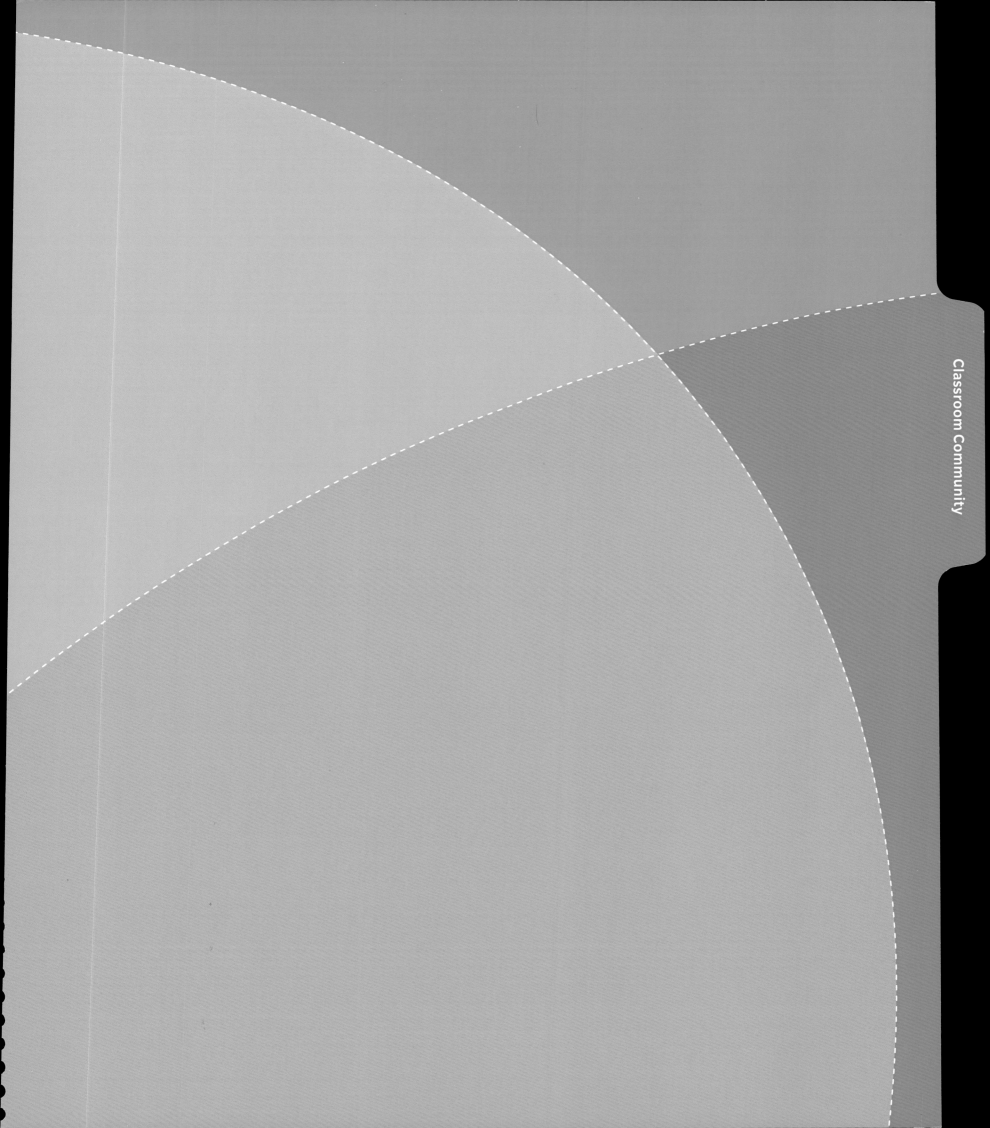
Classroom Community

Classroom Community

Make the Best Use of Your Classroom 112
Get Started with Literacy Centers 114
Embed Social and Emotional Learning 118
Create a Culturally Responsive Environment.. 120
Communicate with Families 122

Classroom Community

Make the Best Use of Your Classroom

Organize your classroom environment with areas for **whole-class** instruction, **small-group** time, and **Literacy Centers**.

 WHOLE CLASS

- Place a large rug on the floor for community building or shared reading.
- Arrange individual desks in groups where children can work in teams or pairs. Allow children to sit on the rug or at their seats during whole-class work.
- Select an area to project videos and other digital resources.
- Use wall space around the community area to display the calendar, messages, and other important content.

 SMALL GROUPS

- Designate a table or area to meet with flexible groups. A table that shifts purposes throughout the day would also work.
- Choose an area away from more collaborative work spaces to help children focus.
- Store Start Right Readers, Tabletop Minilessons, Leveled Readers, instructional cards, and other helpful materials nearby for easy access.

CLASSROOM COMMUNITY

LITERACY CENTERS

- Designate multiple places in the classroom where children can engage in Literacy Center work, such as Word Work, Creativity Corner, and Teamwork Time.
- Create a comfortable space for quiet, independent reading time in the Reading Corner.

See pp. 114–117 for additional information about Literacy Centers.

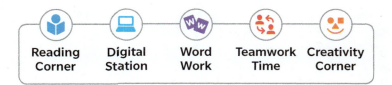

Tips for a More Efficient Classroom

- Determine furniture placement based on traffic flow.
- Allow children to co-create the space at various times during the year.
- Establish systems of expectations and routines to maintain a safe and organized classroom.
- Consider flexible seating, such as sensory seats or beanbag chairs.
- Designate a separate space where children can go to regulate their emotions.
- Provide multiple areas for collaborative or independent work.
- Create a warm environment with natural light and soft colors, when possible.
- Minimize clutter, and be deliberate about what to hang on walls.

Get Started with Literacy Centers

Implement well-defined and organized Literacy Centers to provide children with opportunities to **practice skills**, **make decisions**, and **work cooperatively**.

Set Up Literacy Centers

Use the suggestions on these pages to set up your Literacy Centers for the year. Find the Literacy Center activities on the weekly planning pages in your Teacher's Guide.

Reading Corner | Digital Station | Word Work | Teamwork Time | Creativity Corner

CLASSROOM COMMUNITY

READING CORNER

In the Reading Corner, children practice their reading skills and build motivation and enjoyment of reading by exploring self-selected books, rereading and responding to familiar texts, and reading with peers.

To prepare your Reading Corner,
- designate a quiet, cozy area of the classroom with low open shelves and books that are easy to browse
- include a rug and comfortable seating, such as beanbag chairs, a small couch, or floor pillows
- offer books in a variety of genres, topics, reading levels, and formats, based on children's interests
- include pencils, crayons, markers, and copies of printables children will need, such as the Reading Log

DIGITAL STATION

At the Digital Station, children listen to models of fluent reading and build listening comprehension skills by reading along with eBooks.

To prepare your Digital Station,
- set up a table with electronic devices where children can work without disturbing others
- provide login information and a list of the programs and apps that children may use
- model how to handle and charge computers or tablets
- keep copies of the Listening Log printable at hand and model how to use it
- remind children to wash their hands before and after handling electronic devices

Classroom Community 115

Get Started with Literacy Centers

WORD WORK

In Word Work activities, children review and practice high-frequency words, spelling, and handwriting.

To prepare your Word Work area,
- consider keeping Word Work materials in a box that children can use on any classroom table
- label containers and the materials needed for each activity
- store materials, such as Word Cards, in zipper bags that can be hung on a bulletin board, or in file folders that can be placed in storage bins
- choose a child to help you demonstrate how to complete an activity, thinking aloud as you role-play how to take turns and be a good partner
- model nonexamples, such as speaking too loudly, and then discuss more considerate ways to respond

TEAMWORK TIME

During Teamwork Time activities, children work on an aspect of a module's Inquiry and Research Project. Over the course of a module, children collaborate to generate ideas for, research, complete, and present an inquiry-based project.

To prepare for Teamwork Time,
- gather and set out the materials needed for each stage of the project
- check for understanding of the overall project goals as well as the steps to meet weekly goals
- display a Curiosity Board near the meeting area
- keep children's research questions and their work from each stage of the project to refer to when they make presentations and reflect on their learning

CLASSROOM COMMUNITY

CREATIVITY CORNER

During Creativity Corner activities, children build communication, collaboration, and social and emotional competencies by working together on reading-response activities, participating in Readers' Theater, writing, and creating artwork.

To prepare your Creativity Corner,

- set up an area with a variety of writing, art, and recyclable building materials for children to use at any time
- laminate all the Reading Remake printables and display the one for each week
- designate a visible place for children's work, updating it frequently with their pieces
- take photos of children's work to place in their portfolios or send home

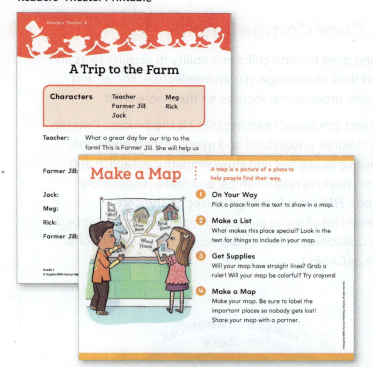

Readers' Theater Printable

Reading Remake Printable

Classroom Community 117

Embed Social and Emotional Learning

Help children develop **social and emotional competencies** that will provide a pathway to academic achievement and a lifetime of success.

● SEL Core Competencies

Learning goes beyond children's ability to acquire facts and expand their knowledge. It is an intellectual, social, and emotional process that focuses on the whole child.

Social and Emotional Learning (SEL) is the process through which children understand and manage their emotions, set positive goals, feel and show empathy, establish and maintain positive relationships, and make responsible decisions. *HMH Into Reading* focuses on the core competencies of social and emotional learning developed by the Collaborative for Academic, Social, and Emotional Learning (CASEL).

● SEL in the Curriculum

Research indicates that integrating SEL into the **daily curriculum** and the **classroom culture** is most effective. This practice fosters transfer of skills because children consistently practice them over time. *HMH Into Reading* focuses on the core SEL competencies through the following program features:

- **SEL Anchor Charts and Lessons**: Display engaging Anchor Charts to introduce a competency and incorporate related activities.
- **Connect to Literature**: In the Teaching Pal and Teacher's Guide, look for connections and prompts to discuss the module focus competency through a text.
- **Inquiry and Research Project**: As children work together on a module Inquiry and Research Project, highlight connections to the Relationship Skills competency.
- **Engagement Routines**: Routines such as Think-Pair-Share and Turn and Talk embedded throughout the program promote the Relationship Skills competency.

SEL Anchor Charts

Program Guide • Grades 1–2

CLASSROOM COMMUNITY

Support Social and Emotional Learning with Texts

Books are powerful tools for teaching social and emotional competencies because they serve as examples and nonexamples of important behaviors, actions, and emotions.

Discussion prompts in your Teaching Pal and Teacher's Guide for the following SEL competencies and texts can help you weave SEL instruction into your daily routine naturally and seamlessly.

Social and Emotional Competency	Grade 1 Texts	Grade 2 Texts
Self-Awareness	The Nest; Blue Bird and Coyote; Step-by-Step Advice from the Animal Kingdom; Monument City; You're a Grand Old Flag; The Contest; Presidents' Day; Try This!; Goal!; I am Amelia Earhart; Pelé, King of Soccer	The Important Book; The Great Fuzz Frenzy; The Puddle Puzzle; A Perfect Season for Dreaming; Recipe for a Fairy Tale; How to Read a Story; Hollywood Chicken; If the Shoe Fits: Two Cinderella Stories; Those Clever Crows
Self-Management	Chicken Little; Interrupting Chicken; The Grasshopper & the Ants; The Tortoise and the Hare; So You Want to Grow a Taco?; The Talking Vegetables; A Year in the Garden; The Curious Garden; Kids Are Inventors, Too!; What Can You Do?; Young Frank Architect; Sky Color; Charlotte the Scientist Is Squished; I am Amelia Earhart	Seed by Seed: The Legend and Legacy of John "Appleseed" Chapman; My Dream Playground; Whoosh!: Lonnie Johnson's Super-Soaking Stream of Inventions; Going Places; Wilma Rudolph: Against All Odds; Who Are Government's Leaders?; Thomas Edison and the Light Bulb; Miss Moore Thought Otherwise; I Am Helen Keller; The Stories He Tells; Drum Dream Girl; The Patchwork Garden; Experiment with What a Plant Needs to Grow; Jack and the Beanstalk; George Washington Carver; The Legend of the Indian Paintbrush
Social Awareness	Kids Speak Up!; Whose Hands Are These?; Dan Had a Plan; Maybe Something Beautiful; Places in My Neighborhood; Who Put the Cookies in the Cookie Jar?; Sam & Dave Dig a Hole; On Meadowview Street; Grand Canyon; Do You Really Want to Visit a Wetland?	We Are Super Citizens; Clark the Shark; The Great Puppy Invasion; Being a Good Citizen; Picture Day Perfection; Get Involved: Be Awesome!; Freddy the Frogcaster; Cloudette; Get Ready for Weather; Whatever the Weather; Dreams Around the World; Where on Earth Is My Bagel?; May Day Around the World; Goal!; Poems in the Attic
Responsible Decision-Making	The Black Rabbit; What Are You Waiting For?; Suki's Kimono; Maybe Something Beautiful; The Talking Vegetables, Sam & Dave Dig a Hole	I Am Helen Keller; Gingerbread for Liberty!; Great Leaders; Get Ready for Weather; Pepita and the Bully; Hollywood Chicken; Drum Dream Girl; Be a Hero! Work It Out!; A Crow, a Lion, and a Mouse! Oh, My!; Roberto Clemente; Jackie and the Beanstalk
Relationship Skills	Pete the Cat: Rocking in My School Shoes; You Will Be My Friend!; My School Trip; A Kids' Guide to Friends; I'm Me!; Suki's Kimono; Good Sports; Baseball Hour; Goal!; The Great Ball Game; If You Plant a Seed; Brontorina	Meet Me Halfway; Big Red Lollipop; Working with Others; Gingerbread for Liberty!; Pepita and the Bully; Nature's Patchwork Quilt: Understanding Habitats; Sea Otter Pups; Abuelo and the Three Bears

Create a Culturally Responsive Environment

Create a classroom environment that **fosters appreciation** and **respect** for all people and cultures.

Embrace Differences

In our diverse society, school should be a place where all children feel **welcomed**, **appreciated**, and **encouraged**. In turn, we should make it a priority to **promote understanding across cultures** and portray the contributions of different groups to the world today.

Consider the following suggestions for promoting a **culturally responsive, antibias environment** for your classroom.

- Teach the ways in which we are the same.
- Point out, judiciously and respectfully, how each student is unique. Emphasize that **differences are to be celebrated**, not glossed over.
- Stay mindful of the fact that certain ways of behaving may have different meanings in different cultures.
- Discuss examples of what it means for children to be **responsible**, **respectful**, and **tolerant citizens** of their community.
- Be mindful of **gender considerations**, reinforcing gender-neutral versions of common words such as *businessperson* or *firefighter*.
- Expose children to books and other learning resources that reflect their **ethnicity**, **culture**, **family structure**, or **socioeconomic status**.
- Educate children about the **history**, **traditions**, and **contributions** of various groups as well as current **social** or **political issues** to expand their knowledge about the world and to give them regular practice with talking about these topics respectfully.

CLASSROOM COMMUNITY

● Honor Home Languages

In today's **multilingual society**, it's increasingly common for children to speak a language other than English at home. Creating links between children's home languages and the English-learning environment at school is key to fostering a sense of belonging. For children who speak only English, the **exposure to other languages** can enhance their listening skills and their ability to think about others' perspectives or points of view.

- **Promote inclusive activities**, such as asking children to share a few words or phrases in their home languages for the entire class to learn.
- **Show respect and appreciation** of your children's home languages by learning a few words yourself.

● Cultural Considerations

In literacy instruction, carefully curated, high-quality texts that **reflect the rich diversity in our school communities** provide natural ways to cultivate a culturally responsive classroom. Make the most of *HMH Into Reading* and *HMH ¡Arriba la Lectura!* through these program features:

- **ethnically diverse literature** that **rejects stereotypes** and reflects the limitless possibilities for all children's future success
- suggested opportunities to share **cultural perspectives** and **language connections**, as in the Text X-Ray feature shown below
- child-centered Inquiry and Research Projects related to **real-world experiences**
- **connections to home and family** through Family Letters in multiple languages

TEXT X-RAY

KEY IDEAS	LANGUAGE
Key Idea pp. 86–87 One haiku poem recalls the joy of eating blueberries, and another pays tribute to corn and delicious foods made from it.	**Ricochet Word** *roly-poly* (p. 90): Some words have just one vowel or consonant that changes, for example: *pitter-patter, teeny-weeny*. These words are fun to say and hear! Explain that *roly-poly* means "round and slightly fat."
Key Idea pp. 88–89 Two more haiku praise the crunchy pecan and the fruit of the prickly pear cactus.	**CULTURAL REFERENCES**
Key Idea p. 90 A final haiku describes the delight of biting into a round, juicy tomato.	*corn* (p. 87): Tell children that scientists think that Native Americans, living in what is now Mexico, developed corn many years ago. Today, it is one of the most important crops in the United States. *dulces* (p. 89): *Dulces* means "sweets" or "candies" in Spanish.

Classroom Community

Communicate with Families

Communicate ways you can work together with families to meet children's learning needs throughout the year.

Introduce Yourself

Starting a school year can be emotional, especially if children are new to your school. Consider these suggestions to **welcome children and their families** into the school community:

- **Mail a letter or postcard** to inform children that you look forward to meeting them.
- **Call parents or caregivers** to introduce yourself and answer their questions.
- **Consider children's home languages.** As you discover families' cultural backgrounds, **provide translations** of any communication in their respective languages, and schedule translators for meetings and conferences.

Meet the Families

Back-to-school night is the perfect time to meet family members. Use the following suggestions to prepare them for the school year:

- **Set expectations** about how often you send letters to families and how and when they can reach you.
- **Convey your homework policy**, stressing the importance of unstructured free time, talking with children, and reading and spending family time together.
- **Display materials** from HMH Into Reading or HMH ¡Arriba la Lectura! for parents to browse through, and explain the curriculum.
- **Introduce volunteer opportunities**, explaining how families can get involved throughout the year.

CLASSROOM COMMUNITY

Foster Ongoing Outreach

Encourage family members to be active participants in their child's learning. These suggestions will help parents understand expectations and feel confident about their roles:

- **Send home the Family Letter** printable at the beginning of each module to inform families about the topics and skills children are learning and to offer practical ideas for reinforcing them. Family Letters are available in **English**, **Spanish**, **Haitian Creole**, and **Portuguese**.
- **Host family workshops** on specific aspects of support for children at home, such as social and emotional learning, oral language development, shared and independent reading strategies, writing opportunities, and summer learning.
- **Organize special events** for families to view their child's projects and presentations.

Share Progress

Use the following suggestions during **parent-teacher conferences** to **share children's development** and discuss strategies for working together:

- Focus on the child's particular **strengths and progress** since the last meeting.
- Share the child's reading, writing, and other **learning goals**.
- Review the child's **portfolio** to look at samples of his or her classwork showing growth.
- Share **assessment scores** and individual reports.
- **Keep a log** to record important notes about parent communications and areas that require follow-up.

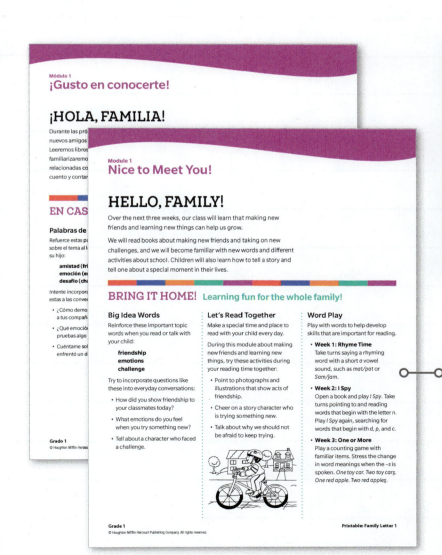

Student Growth Report

FAMILY LETTERS
Available in English, Spanish, Haitian Creole, and Portuguese

Notes

¡Arriba la Lectura!

¡Arriba la Lectura!

Welcome to *HMH ¡Arriba la Lectura!*	126
Hispanic and Universal Literature	128
Dual Language Program Planning	134

¡Arriba la Lectura!

Welcome to HMH ¡Arriba la Lectura!

HMH ¡Arriba la Lectura! is a **comprehensive Spanish literacy** and **language arts program** with research-based instruction designed to support the linguistic and academic growth of **multilingual learners**.

Endorsed by a Renowned Author Team

HMH ¡Arriba la Lectura! was developed by the same panel of authors and advisors who guided the instructional design of HMH Into Reading, as well as three experts in the field of Spanish-language acquisition and dual language learning. Their collective review of all literature and authorship of select program features and components has assured an offering of culturally and developmentally appropriate content for teachers and children.

Alma Flor Ada, Ph.D.
Dr. Ada, Professor Emerita at the University of San Francisco, is an expert in the field of literature and biliteracy. She has authored more than 200 award-winning books—academic titles, as well as works for children and young adults—and is a thought leader and advisor in the area of transformative education.

F. Isabel Campoy, M.A., Lic.
Ms. Campoy is a celebrated bilingual author of more than 150 children's books. An internationally renowned academic, teacher, and translator, Ms. Campoy is also a member of the Academia Norteamericana de la Lengua Española.

Elena Izquierdo, Ph.D.
In addition to being Associate Professor of Teacher Training at the University of Texas at El Paso, Dr. Izquierdo is a professional researcher with a focus on dual language learning and teaching, biliteracy, and educational equity for English learners.

¡ARRIBA LA LECTURA!

Authentic Curriculum

Designed for biliteracy and dual language settings, *HMH ¡Arriba la Lectura!* is fully equitable to *HMH Into Reading*. It has been carefully adapted to include **authentic and original Spanish literature** and to provide pedagogically sound **Spanish language instruction**. This parallel curriculum assures an **equitable** learning experience for language learners of all backgrounds, using **authentic Spanish teaching methodologies**.

Foundational Skills Instruction

- **Phonological awareness** and **phonics** lessons follow **authentic, systematic methods and routines** for teaching the Spanish letter-sound system and the syllabic nature of the language.
- The scope and sequence is informed by best practices in **Spanish phonics instruction**.

Spelling Instruction

- Spelling lessons reinforce the **reciprocal nature of decoding** (phonics) **and encoding** (spelling).
- Instruction builds on **syllabic awareness** and what learners know about **Spanish sound-letter relationships** to help all children master **Spanish spelling rules**, including those of the written accent.
- Guidance is provided for teachers to construct **authentic** *dictados*, or **dictation mentor texts**, as a strategy for reviewing and reinforcing the fundamentals of Spanish mechanics.

Grammar Instruction

- The **breadth and sequence** of grammar topics is suitable to Spanish. Lessons provide **in-depth explanations** of essential concepts, including these:
  - gender-number agreement
  - augmentatives and diminutives
  - rules of capitalization and punctuation
  - verb mood and tense
  - implicit subject work

Guía del maestro

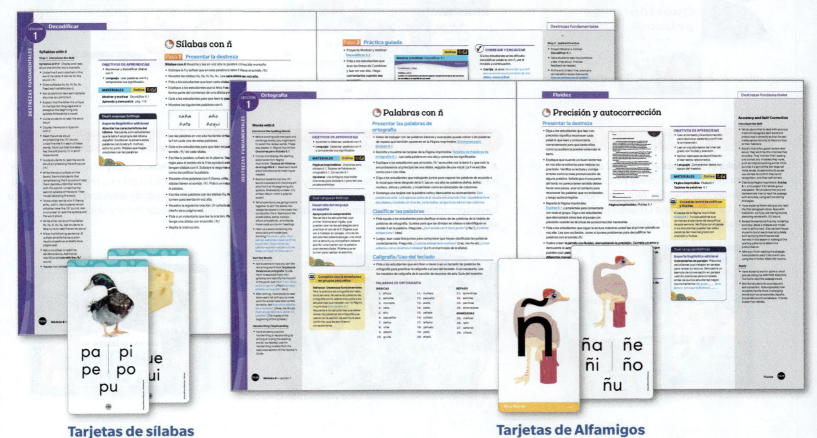

Tarjetas de sílabas y ortografía

Tarjetas de Alfamigos

¡Arriba la Lectura! 127

Hispanic and Universal Literature

HMH ¡Arriba la Lectura! takes an additive approach to developing bilingualism in children and puts into readers' hands a variety of texts originally written in Spanish, selected for their **literary caliber, cultural relevance,** and **universal appeal.**

Student Literature Resources

A rich variety of classical and contemporary Spanish-language texts underscores the vast heritage and heterogenous nature of the Spanish-speaking world. Additional multicultural, multigenre texts support instruction that is culturally responsive and inclusive of a diverse audience.

*mi*Libro

Authentic Spanish texts within the student *mi*Libro include a variety of genres and topics relevant to children's lives.

Lecturas iniciales

Decodable texts originally written in Spanish give emerging readers in Grades K–2 weekly practice for mastering new and previously learned phonic elements.

Authentic Poems in Spanish

Original poems **written by Alma Flor Ada, F. Isabel Campoy,** and other **notable Hispanic poets** support children's acquisition of Spanish phonemic awareness and phonics skills.

Superlibros

Big Books of Rhymes and **El ABC de Culebra** developed expressly for Grade K *HMH ¡Arriba la Lectura!* by Alma Flor Ada and F. Isabel Campoy expose children to the sounds and cadence of Spanish.

Revista Aventuras

A series of books with a variety of high-interest, topically relevant texts originally written in Spanish target language development and reading comprehension skills.

Videos de cierre/de la selección

Selection Videos, many of which are unique to *HMH ¡Arriba la Lectura!*, present topics and themes in engaging ways and help to develop children's media literacy skills.

AUTHENTIC LITERATURE See the following pages for a list of authentic and culturally relevant texts in HMH ¡Arriba la Lectura!, Grades 1–2.

¡ARRIBA LA LECTURA!

Teacher Literature Resources

The HMH ¡Arriba la Lectura! teacher materials honor the needs of teachers and children in dual language and biliteracy classrooms.

Guía del maestro

NUESTRA LENGUA ES ARTE
Located in the Teacher's Guide, this collection of poems and short stories originally written in Spanish can be read aloud to children at the end of each module to improve listening comprehension and foster literary appreciation.

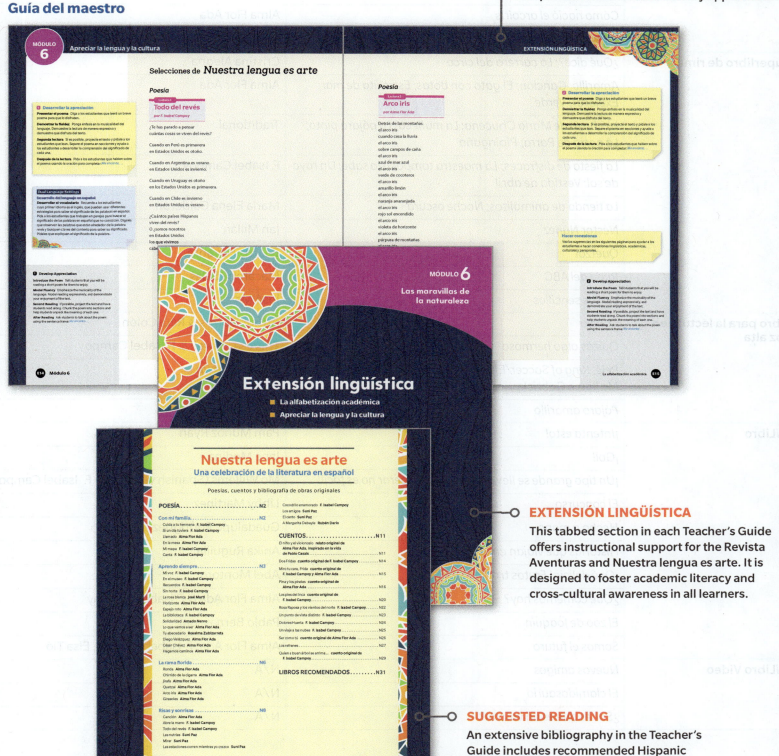

EXTENSIÓN LINGÜÍSTICA
This tabbed section in each Teacher's Guide offers instructional support for the Revista Aventuras and Nuestra lengua es arte. It is designed to foster academic literacy and cross-cultural awareness in all learners.

SUGGESTED READING
An extensive bibliography in the Teacher's Guide includes recommended Hispanic readings, classified by genre, to consider for your classroom library.

¡Arriba la Lectura! 129

Hispanic and Universal Literature

Use this table as a reference for the Grade 1 authentic Spanish literature.

Grade 1		
Component	**Title**	**Author**
Superlibro	*Aunque viva en el agua*	Antonio Mignucci
	La asombrosa vida de las mariposas monarca	Ángela Calderón
	Cómo nació el arcoíris	Alma Flor Ada
	Superlibro de rimas	F. Isabel Campoy & Alma Flor Ada
Superlibro de rimas	*¿Qué dice?; La carrera del circo*	Cristina Alegría
	Amarillo; Canción; El gato con botas; Estrellita de mar; Explorar; Verde	Alma Flor Ada
	La choza de María Chucena; La muñeca; La pájara pinta; La perra de Parra; Pipirigaña	Traditional
	La fiesta de disfraces; La maestra tampoco lo sabe; Un rayo de sol; Vestida de abril	F. Isabel Campoy
	La tienda de animalitos; Noche oscura	María Elena Calderón
	Néstor Núñez	Jan Millán
	Quetzal	Beatriz Ferrante
	Rima del ABC	Macarena Salas
	Versos sencillos	José Martí
Libro para la lectura en voz alta	*Abuela*	Arthur Dorros & Raúl Colón
	Quizás algo hermoso	Theresa Howell & F. Isabel Campoy
	Pelé, King of Soccer/El rey del fútbol; My Name is Gabriela/Me llamo Gabriela	Monica Brown
	Pájaro amarillo	Olga de Dios
***mi*Libro**	*¡Intenta esto!*	Pam Muñoz Ryan
	¡Gol!	Jane Medina
	¡Un tipo grande se llevó mi pelota!; ¡Esperar no es fácil!	Mo Willems (Spanish version by F. Isabel Campoy)
	El concurso	Libby Martinez
	Hecho a mano	Guadalupe Rodríguez
	Historias que viajan en el tiempo	Anika Ruguilla
	¡Qué delicia! Frutas tropicales	Abel Montoro
	¿Qué comemos hoy?	Alma Flor Ada & F. Isabel Campoy
	El zoo de Joaquín	Pablo Bernasconi
	Somos el futuro	Alma Flor Ada, F. Isabel Campoy, Elsa Tió
***mi*Libro Video**	*Nuevos amigos*	N/A
	El clamidosaurio	N/A
	¿Sabes qué es un volcán?	N/A

Grade 1 continued		
Component	**Title**	**Author**
Extensión lingüística	*Caracola*	Federico García Lorca
	Picnic, ¡allá vamos!	María Cáceres
	Bilingüe; Abuelita; Más poderoso que yo; Más que el oro; Pares; Viento, viento; El león y el chapulín; Clementina; Geranios; Los patines nuevos	Alma Flor Ada
	De paseo por el barrio	Ana Di Mare
	¡Hola! Me llamo Manuela; Pablo y Diego; Domingo por la mañana; Una enorme familia; Los peores dragones para mí; Caras de calabaza; Viajar; Chocolate; Veinte cestas; Cómo imaginar a un extraterrestre; La punta de mi lápiz	F. Isabel Campoy
	Vida en el campo, vida en la ciudad	Luciano Saracino
	Cirilo, el cocodrilo	Almudena Taboada
	Los animales y sus ambientes	N/A
	¡Como perro y gato!	Lucía Pierri
	Animales protectores	Gabriela Fluker
	Hojas, nieve, flores y playa: Las estaciones	Anita Tower
	Las estaciones y la naturaleza	Morena Sanz
	Cómo hacer un tambor; Todo tiene música	Aida Oreiro
	La selva tropical y sus habitantes	María Wos
	Nuevos amigos	Marilú Levi
	Cuello duro	Elsa Bornemann
	Momentos felices	Alma Flor Ada & Graciela Lecube-Chavez
	La germinación	Cecilia Pisos
	¡Vuela, Mariposa! ¡Vuela!	Lydia Giménez Llort
	Mosquito	Guadalupe Castellano
Revista Aventuras	*¿Los insectos hablan?; Amigos para siempre*	Carola Sony
	Cómo crece el maíz; La foca Andre	Anita Tower
	El ratoncito y el león	Alma Flor Ada
	La amistad	F. Isabel Campoy & Gloria Fuertes
	La vida de los árboles	Anonymous
	Manual para soñar	Cristina Núñez Pereira & Rafael R. Varcárcel
	Música en el tren	María Wos
	Pequeña historia del libro	Mora Hynes
	Trabajo en equipo	Isabel Stern
	Una visita al zoo	Aida Oreiro

Hispanic and Universal Literature

Use this table as a reference for the Grade 2 authentic Spanish literature.

Grade 2

Component	Title	Author
Libro para la lectura en voz alta	Mango, Abuela y yo	Meg Medina
	Ramiro el cuentista	Paz Rodero
	Ricitos de Oro y los tres dinosaurios	Spanish version by F. Isabel Campoy
	Un tiempo perfecto para soñar	Benjamín Alire Sáenz
	Juana Inés	Georgina Lázaro
	Pedacitos de huerto	Diane de Anda
miLibro	El desfile de las nubes; Amiga hormiga	Alma Flor Ada
	El agua rueda, el agua sube	Pat Mora
	Pepita y la peleonera	Ofelia Dumas Lachtman
	Frida Kahlo	F. Isabel Campoy
	Tiempo al Tiempo: El color del agua / Dragones de nubes	Alma Flor Ada & Pat Mora
	La niña que soñaba con tambores	Margarita Engle (illustrated by Rafael López)
	Abuelo y los tres osos	Jerry Tello
	Mi casa: la naturaleza	Alberto Blanco, Alma Flor Ada, F. Isabel Campoy
	¡Gol!	Sean Taylor
miLibro Video	Roberto Clemente	N/A
Texto de enfoque	El gran capoquero	Lynne Cherry (translated by Alma Flor Ada)
Extensión lingüística	El ABC de mi escuela; Voy a ir de paseo; Juega conmigo; Un alto precio; El cuervo y las plumas del pavo real; ¡Vamos, vamos!; Yo soy poeta; Las cabritas porfiadas; Vendaval; El beso; Alto, bien alto; Tú eres muy rico; La calle donde vivo; Celebración ¡cha'an!	F. Isabel Campoy
	En el gallinero; Faro; Verde; Zorra y zorrillo; El palacio de malaquita; Mi familia; Gotas de lluvia; El cumpleaños de Serafina; Abeja; Lilí, Loló y Lulú; Canción de todos los niños y niñas del mundo; El mismo sol	Alma Flor Ada
	La escuela	Meritxell Martí
	Un encargo insignificante	Pedro Pablo Sacristán
	Huellas en caminos blancos	Marilú Finn

Grade 2 continued

Component	Title	Author
Extensión lingüística continued	Extrañas sombras	Daniel Nesquens
	La leyenda del fuego	Francisco Alén Freire
	La paca y el escarabajo	Traditional
	Gabriela Mistral, la poeta de los niños	Ailén Espino
	La cigarra y la hormiga; El maíz más preciado	Elsie Mei
	Hablar con las manos; Cómo hacer un abanico de papel	Ana di Mare
	Louis Braille	Mora Hynes
	Una huerta en casa	Marilú Fin
	Una cuncuna amarilla	María de la Luz Corcuera
	El talento de la oruga	Diana Benavente
	El arte de hacer amigos	Amy Blas
Revista Aventuras	¡Quiero ayudar!; Faro	Alma Flor Ada
	Ayudantes increíbles; Un perro en casa	Núria Roca
	El elefante bebé	Jezabel Janáriz
	El tiburón blanco; La música	Marcos Salvador Blanco
	El zapatero y los duendes; Los arrecifes de coral	Pablo Ernesto Flores
	Estaba la rana; La voz del niño; Las palomitas del campo; Los pollitos dicen	Traditional
	Los caballitos de mar	Francisca Nolte
	Tiempo Mateo	Lamar Ordenario
	Todas las buenas manos	F. Isabel Campoy
	Una cuncuna amarilla	María de la Luz Corcuera

Dual Language Program Planning

When paired in dual language settings, *HMH ¡Arriba la Lectura!* and *HMH Into Reading* comprise an academically rigorous, culturally relevant, and pedagogically sound **biliteracy curriculum** designed to assure student mastery of language and content.

● Systematically Connect Programs to Build Biliteracy

High-interest, knowledge-building modules in *HMH ¡Arriba la Lectura!* and *HMH Into Reading* follow a **parallel structure**, ensuring equal access to content and **fluid transitions between both languages**.

Concrete suggestions and planning tools in the complementary **Dual Language Implementation Guide** facilitate the choosing and combining of content from both programs according to teachers' dual language model needs.

Complementary resources to reinforce rich cross-curricular content and language learning in English and Spanish

Skill and concept development aligns across programs, except where linguistic differences necessitate instructional differences

Dual language planning tools to help choose and combine content from both programs

¡ARRIBA LA LECTURA!

Dual Language Supports in *HMH ¡Arriba la Lectura!*

HMH ¡Arriba la Lectura! offers ample and rich opportunities for building **multilingual learners' metalinguistic awareness** and **metacognitive skills**. A daily Dual Language Settings feature in the Teacher's Guide provides strategies for guiding children to make cross-language connections and extend their knowledge of Spanish through additional readings of authentic text.

PUENTE INTERLINGÜÍSTICO
Cross-Linguistic Bridge provides strategies for helping dual language learners engage in contrastive analysis of Spanish and English, with a focus on vocabulary, grammar, phonetic elements, and concepts of print.

Guía del maestro

Dual Language Settings

Puente interlingüístico: Lectura, Vocabulario y Destrezas fundamentales

Mural bilingüe de Palabras que quiero saber Trabaje con la clase para crear un Mural bilingüe de palabras que completarán a lo largo de todo el módulo durante el tiempo de trabajo en grupos pequeños. Usen este Mural para anotar las Palabras que quiero saber del módulo, junto con sus equivalentes en inglés. Si lo desea, anote los pares de cognados en un mismo color o anótelos también en la Tabla de cognados. Si los niños desean participar, permítales que escriban ellos mismos las palabras o que hagan un dibujo al lado de los pares de palabras.

Semejanzas lingüísticas: Vocabulario del lector: *conversación colaborativa, lenguaje formal, lenguaje informal* Repase con los niños el vocabulario que aprendieron en esta lección y pida a algunos voluntarios que digan sus equivalentes en inglés o dígalos usted: *conversación colaborativa-collaborative conversation, lenguaje formal-formal language, lenguaje informal-informal language*. Pregunte a los niños si creen que algunos de estos pares de palabras son parecidos en español y en inglés. Anote esas palabras en la Tabla de cognados de la clase. **TRANSLANGUAGING**

Semejanzas lingüísticas: Destreza de estrategias de vocabulario: Antónimos Recuerde a los niños que, tanto en inglés como en español, los antónimos son palabras con significados opuestos. Señale que las palabras *antónimo* y *antonym* son cognados. Dé un ejemplo de antónimos en español. *Las palabras fuerte y débil son antónimos, porque significan dos cosas opuestas.* Pida a un voluntario que dé un ejemplo de dos antónimos en inglés. Luego, pregunte: *¿Son las palabras en inglés slow y fast antónimos?* (sí) *¿Por qué?* (porque una significa lo contrario de la otra) *¿Son las palabras high y tall antónimos?* (no) *¿Por qué?* (porque tienen el mismo significado)
TRANSLANGUAGING

Diferencias lingüísticas: Palabras de uso frecuente: *animal, árbol, carnívoro, especie, pequeño* Las palabras de uso frecuente varían mucho en inglés y en español. Repase con los niños las Palabras de uso frecuente de esta semana. Escriba *árbol* en el Mural bilingüe de Palabras que quiero saber. Pregunte a los niños: *¿Alguien sabe cómo se dice árbol en inglés?* (tree) *¡Muy bien! ¿Creen que estas dos palabras se parecen?* (no) *Entonces, anotaré árbol con un color distinto.* Repita con las otras Palabras que quiero saber. Recuerde a los niños que van a usar un mismo color para los pares de palabras que son cognados. Si lo desea, también puede anotar las palabras que sean cognados en el Mural de cognados de la clase.

Extensión lingüística

Profundizar la apreciación y la comprensión Use la Lección 5 de la Semana 1 de la sección de Extensión lingüística que se encuentra al final de esta Guía del maestro.

EXTENSIÓN LINGÜÍSTICA
Language Extensions directs teachers to additional lessons centered around culturally relevant texts originally written in Spanish and intended to foster literary appreciation and language development in learners of all proficiency levels.

Dual Language Program Planning

● Dual Language Implementation Guide

Conceived by program author and biliteracy expert Dr. Elena Izquierdo, this teachers' companion was developed to ensure a flexible and efficient implementation of *HMH ¡Arriba la Lectura!* and *HMH Into Reading* that takes into account the diverse and varying nature of today's multilingual classrooms and education models.

The three-part guide satisfies three aspects of the multilayered needs of dual language teachers: professional learning materials, biliteracy planning resources, and authentic biliteracy evaluation tools.

PART 1

Language Acquisition in Bilingual Environments is designed to provide **ongoing professional learning** support for dual language practitioners and in-depth information on topics such as **contrastive analysis**, **translanguaging**, and **metalanguage**.

Dual Language Implementation Guide

○ **RESEARCH-BACKED ARTICLES**
Reinforce or extend what you already know about biliteracy development strategies, such as contrastive analysis, translanguaging, and family/community involvement.

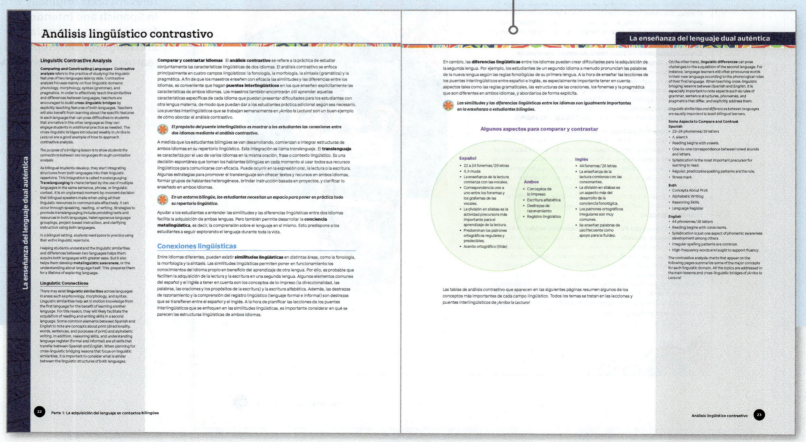

Program Guide • Grades 1–2

¡ARRIBA LA LECTURA!

Dual Language Implementation Guide

Modelos diversos con principios comunes

Diverse Models with Common Principles
Bilingual Models The terms *biliteracy*, *bilingual education*, and even *dual language* can be applied to many different types of programs that provide literacy and content instruction to all students through two languages. However, the diverse models are all based on the same principles: they all promote bilingualism and biliteracy while encouraging identity development, cross-cultural competence, and multicultural appreciation.

Dual Language Models
Dual language models integrate language and academic content instruction. Goals include bilingualism and biliteracy, academic achievement in two languages, and appreciation of different cultures.

The following are some of the most common school models applied throughout the U.S. Determining which model is most appropriate depends on the population of the school and the district's requirements.

According to the **composition of the class**, that is, how many students in the class speak Spanish and how many speak English, programs are divided into two categories:

One-Way Program
- Typically, at least two thirds of the students are proficient or dominant speakers of either English or the partner language.
- At least half the instruction time is spent in the partner language, but it could account for up to 90% of the time in the early grades.
- There is a distinct separation of the two languages, accompanied by intentionally designed bridge lessons.

Two-Way Program
- Typically, half of the students are proficient or dominant English speakers while the other half are proficient or dominant speakers of the partner...

Modelos bilingües Los términos *biliteracidad*, *educación bilingüe* e incluso *doble inmersión* pueden aplicarse a muchos tipos diferentes de programas de enseñanza de lectoescritura y contenido académico que se imparten a todos los estudiantes en dos idiomas. Sin embargo, estos modelos diversos están fundados en los mismos principios: todos promueven el bilingüismo y la biliteracidad a la vez que fomentan el desarrollo de la identidad, la competencia intercultural y la comprensión multicultural.

Modelos de lenguaje dual

Los modelos de lenguaje dual integran la enseñanza de la lengua y el contenido académico. Entre los objetivos, se incluyen el bilingüismo y la biliteracidad, el rendimiento académico en dos lenguas y la apreciación de diferentes culturas.

A continuación, se detallan algunos de los modelos escolares más comunes en Estados Unidos. Para elegir el modelo más adecuado según las circunstancias, hay que tener en cuenta la población estudiantil de la escuela y los requisitos del distrito.

Según **la composición de la clase**, es decir, cuántos estudiantes hablan español y cuántos hablan inglés, los programas se dividen en dos categorías:

Programa unidireccional	Programa bidireccional
• Por lo general, al menos dos tercios de los estudiantes son hablantes competentes de inglés o de la lengua asociada, o demuestran un buen dominio en cualquiera de las dos lenguas.	• Por lo general, la mitad de los estudiantes son hablantes competentes de inglés o tienen buen dominio de la lengua, mientras que la otra mitad tienen esas destrezas en la lengua asociada.
• Al menos la mitad del tiempo de clase se dicta en la lengua asociada, aunque en los grados inferiores podría extenderse al 90 % del tiempo de clase.	• No menos de un tercio y no más de dos tercios de la clase es monolingüe o tiene buen dominio de cualquiera de las dos lenguas.
• Hay una separación bien marcada de los dos idiomas, acompañada de lecciones de puente diseñadas de forma intencional.	• Al menos la mitad del tiempo de clase es en la lengua asociada, aunque en los primeros grados podría extenderse al 90 %.
	• Hay una separación bien marcada de los dos idiomas, acompañada de lecciones de puente diseñadas de forma intencional.

BACKGROUND INFORMATION
Access information about the importance of multilingual education and different types of bilingual education models.

Glosario en español

Desarrollar un vocabulario compartido Las definiciones de este glosario reflejan usos comunes actuales. Existen diferencias significativas en el uso de los términos por parte de distintos educadores, principalmente porque el lenguaje dual y la biliteracidad son campos de estudio que todavía se encuentran en desarrollo y expansión. El propósito de este glosario es contribuir a la estandarización de una terminología básica compartida.

A
adquisición del lenguaje Trayectoria del desarrollo del lenguaje en los estudiantes que adquieren una primera y una segunda lengua; incluye lenguaje tanto receptivo como expresivo **En inglés:** *language acquisition*

análisis contrastivo Práctica pedagógica en la que los estudiantes comparan y contrastan la morfología, la fonología, la sintaxis, la gramática y la pragmática de la lengua mayoritaria y de la lengua asociada **En inglés:** *contrastive analysis*

B
bilingüismo Capacidad de una persona para comunicarse en dos idiomas; el nivel del dominio de las destrezas para escuchar, hablar, leer y escribir en cada idioma puede ser muy variable en cada individuo y puede abarcar un amplio rango, desde un dominio nulo o muy básico de algunas destrezas en el segundo idioma hasta un dominio total de ambos idiomas. **En inglés:** *bilingualism*

biliteracidad Desarrollo de la lectoescritura en dos idiomas, lo que incluye todas las competencias lingüísticas, es decir, la comprensión auditiva, la lectura, la escritura y la expresión oral; también conocida como *alfabetización bilingüe* y *lectoescritura bilingüe* **En inglés:** *biliteracy*

C
capacidad oral Todas las destrezas de expresión oral y comprensión auditiva que se usan en el lenguaje oral. La capacidad oral es una de las bases fundamentales para la lectoescritura. **En inglés:** *oracy*

cartel didáctico Representación visual de conceptos o del contenido de una lección expresados con dibujos y/o un lenguaje sencillo, a menudo creado por el maestro en colaboración con los estudiantes **En inglés:** *anchor chart*

cognados Palabras que suenan y se escriben de forma similar en dos idiomas, y tienen la misma raíz **En inglés:** *cognates*

conciencia metalingüística Comprensión de cómo funciona una lengua y cómo cambia en diferentes situaciones. En relación a un estudiante bilingüe, la conciencia metalingüística se refiere a la comprensión de las similitudes y diferencias entre los dos idiomas **En inglés:** *metalinguistic awareness*

D
dictado Estrategia de enseñanza en la que el maestro dicta palabras u oraciones relacionadas con los textos o destrezas que los estudiantes están aprendiendo; a lo largo de varios días, los estudiantes abordan el mismo dictado mediante distintas modalidades que re... competencias lingüísticas (comprensión auditi... escritura). El dictado puede usarse como herra... desarrollo del lenguaje y de destrezas específic... biliteracidad, también puede usarse para hace... **En inglés:** *dictado*

E
efectividad Eficacia; facultad de alcanzar un ... el hecho de que se obtienen mejores resultado... lenguaje dual y de biliteracidad en comparació... exclusivamente en inglés **En inglés:** *efficacy*

equidad Igualdad y justicia; en educación, se ... todos los estudiantes a una enseñanza eficaz c... materiales adecuados de alta calidad, independ... instrucción **En inglés:** *equity*

escritor emergente Escritor que se encuentr... adquisición de las destrezas de escritura; tam... principiante **En inglés:** *emergent writer*

evidencia Información confiable basada en la ... incorpora a las decisiones relacionadas con la e...

F
falsos cognados Palabras que suenan o se es... dos idiomas, pero que tienen significados dife... confusiones; también conocidos como *falsos a...*

H
hablante de herencia Estudiante cuya prime... mayoritaria, pero que ha crecido en un hogar o ... lengua asociada. En general, los hablantes de h... destrezas lingüísticas receptivas y expresivas e... lengua dominante es la mayoritaria y ha recibid... ella. **En inglés:** *heritage speaker*

L
lector emergente Lector que se encuentra e... adquisición de las destrezas de lectura; tambié... principiante **En inglés:** *emergent reader*

GLOSSARY
Refer to Spanish and English glossaries of biliteracy terms.

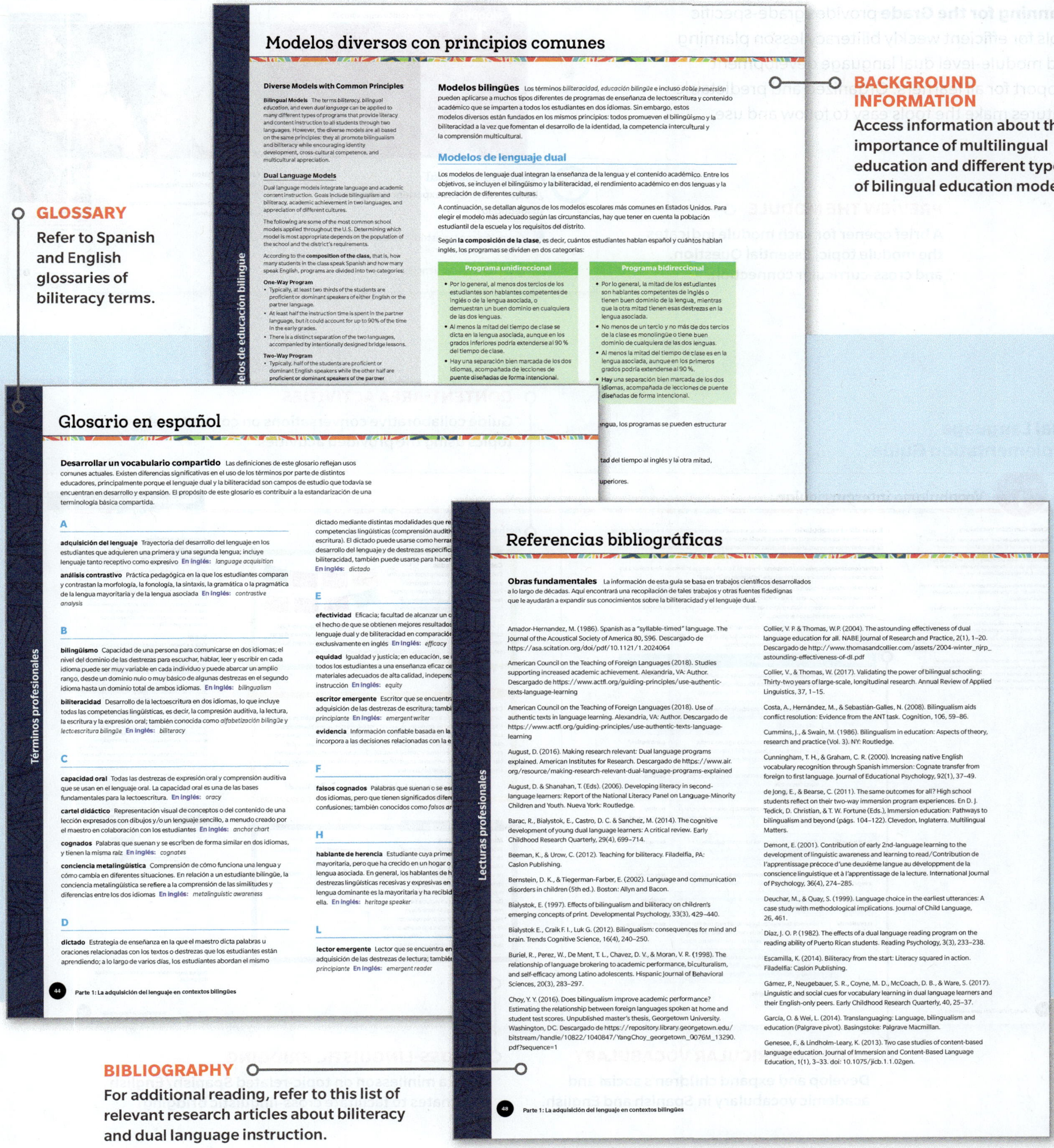

Referencias bibliográficas

Obras fundamentales La información de esta guía se basa en trabajos científicos desarrollados a lo largo de décadas. Aquí encontrará una recopilación de tales trabajos y otras fuentes fidedignas que le ayudarán a expandir sus conocimientos sobre la biliteracidad y el lenguaje dual.

Amador-Hernandez, M. (1986). Spanish as a "syllable-timed" language. The Journal of the Acoustical Society of America 80, S96. Descargado de https://asa.scitation.org/doi/pdf/10.1121/1.2024064

American Council on the Teaching of Foreign Languages (2018). Studies supporting increased academic achievement. Alexandria, VA: Author. Descargado de https://www.actfl.org/guiding-principles/use-authentic-texts-language-learning

American Council on the Teaching of Foreign Languages (2018). Use of authentic texts in language learning. Alexandria, VA: Author. Descargado de https://www.actfl.org/guiding-principles/use-authentic-texts-language-learning

August, D. (2016). Making research relevant: Dual language programs explained. American Institutes for Research. Descargado de https://www.air.org/resource/making-research-relevant-dual-language-programs-explained

August, D. & Shanahan, T. (Eds.) (2006). Developing literacy in second-language learners: Report of the National Literacy Panel on Language-Minority Children and Youth. Nueva York: Routledge.

Barac, R., Bialystok, E., Castro, D. C. & Sanchez, M. (2014). The cognitive development of young dual language learners: A critical review. Early Childhood Research Quarterly, 29(4), 699–714.

Beeman, K., & Urow, C. (2012). Teaching for biliteracy. Filadelfia, PA: Caslon Publishing.

Bernstein, D. K., & Tiegerman-Farber, E. (2002). Language and communication disorders in children (5th ed.). Boston: Allyn and Bacon.

Bialystok, E. (1997). Effects of bilingualism and bilingualism on children's emerging concepts of print. Developmental Psychology, 33(3), 429–440.

Bialystok E., Craik F. I., Luk G. (2012). Bilingualism: consequences for mind and brain. Trends Cognitive Science, 16(4), 240–250.

Buriel, R., Perez, W., De Ment, T. L., Chavez, D. V., & Moran, V. R. (1998). The relationship of language brokering to academic performance, biculturalism, and self-efficacy among Latino adolescents. Hispanic Journal of Behavioral Sciences, 20(3), 283–297.

Choy, Y. Y. (2016). Does bilingualism improve academic performance? Estimating the relationship between foreign languages spoken at home and student test scores. Unpublished master's thesis, Georgetown University. Washington, DC. Descargado de https://repository.library.georgetown.edu/bitstream/handle/10822/1040847/YangChoy_georgetown_0076M_13290.pdf?sequence=1

Collier, V. P. & Thomas, W.P. (2004). The astounding effectiveness of dual language education for all. NABE Journal of Research and Practice, 2(1), 1–20. Descargado de http://www.thomasandcollier.com/assets/2004-winter_njrp_astounding-effectiveness-of-dl.pdf

Collier, V., & Thomas, W. (2017). Validating the power of bilingual schooling: Thirty-two years of large-scale, longitudinal research. Annual Review of Applied Linguistics, 37, 1–15.

Costa, A., Hernández, M., & Sebastián-Gallés, N. (2008). Bilingualism aids conflict resolution: Evidence from the ANT task. Cognition, 106, 59–86.

Cummins, J., & Swain, M. (1986). Bilingualism in education: Aspects of theory, research and practice (Vol. 3). NY: Routledge.

Cunningham, T. H., & Graham, C. R. (2000). Increasing native English vocabulary recognition through Spanish immersion: Cognate transfer from foreign to first language. Journal of Educational Psychology, 92(1), 37–49.

de Jong, E., & Bearse, C. (2011). The same outcomes for all? High school students reflect on their two-way immersion program experiences. En D. J. Tedick, D. Christian, & T. W. Fortune (Eds.), Immersion education: Pathways to bilingualism and beyond (págs. 104–122). Clevedon, Inglaterra. Multilingual Matters.

Demont, E. (2001). Contribution of early 2nd-language learning to the development of linguistic awareness and learning to read/Contribution de l'apprentissage précoce d'une deuxième langue au développement de la conscience linguistique et à l'apprentissage de la lecture. International Journal of Psychology, 36(4), 274–285.

Deuchar, M., & Quay, S. (1999). Language choice in the earliest utterances: A case study with methodological implications. Journal of Child Language, 26, 461.

Díaz, J. O. P. (1982). The effects of a dual language reading program on the reading ability of Puerto Rican students. Reading Psychology, 3(3), 233–238.

Escamilla, K. (2014). Biliteracy from the start: Literacy squared in action. Filadelfia: Caslon Publishing.

Gámez, P., Neugebauer, S. R., Coyne, M. D., McCoach, D. B., & Ware, S. (2017). Linguistic and social cues for vocabulary learning in dual language learners and their English-only peers. Early Childhood Research Quarterly, 40, 25–37.

García, O. & Wei, L. (2014). Translanguaging: Language, bilingualism and education (Palgrave pivot). Basingstoke: Palgrave Macmillan.

Genesee, F., & Lindholm-Leary, K. (2013). Two case studies of content-based language education. Journal of Immersion and Content-Based Language Education, 1(1), 3–33. doi: 10.1075/jicb.1.1.02gen.

BIBLIOGRAPHY
For additional reading, refer to this list of relevant research articles about biliteracy and dual language instruction.

¡Arriba la Lectura! 137

Dual Language Program Planning

PART 2

Planning for the Grade provides grade-specific tools for efficient weekly biliteracy lesson planning and module-level dual language development support for all learners. Organized and predictable features make the tools easy to follow and use.

PREVIEW THE MODULE
A brief opener for each module indicates the module topic, Essential Question, and cross-curricular connection.

Dual Language Implementation Guide

CONTENT-AREA ACTIVITIES
Guide collaborative conversations on content-area topics using the provided activities.

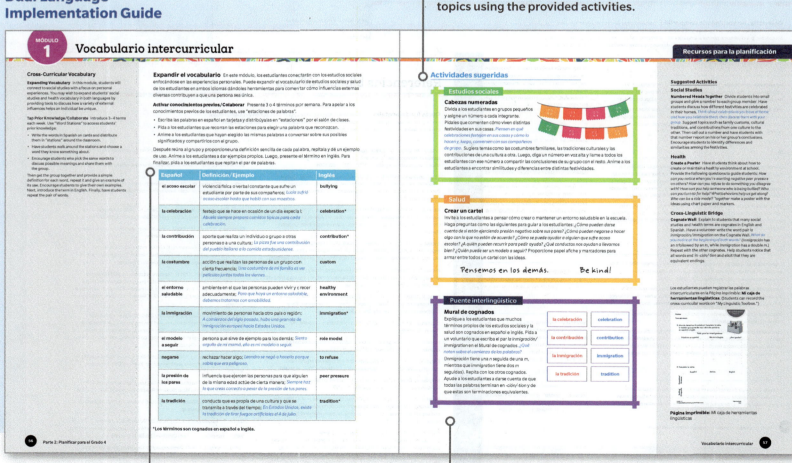

CROSS-CURRICULAR VOCABULARY
Develop and expand children's social and academic vocabulary in Spanish and English.

CROSS-LINGUISTIC BRIDGING
Use a minilesson on topic-related Spanish/English cognates to facilitate cross-linguistic bridging.

Program Guide • Grades 1–2

¡ARRIBA LA LECTURA!

Dual Language Implementation Guide

BILITERACY AT A GLANCE
Use weekly planning charts to purposefully determine what content and skills from *HMH ¡Arriba la Lectura!* and *HMH Into Reading* to teach in each language.

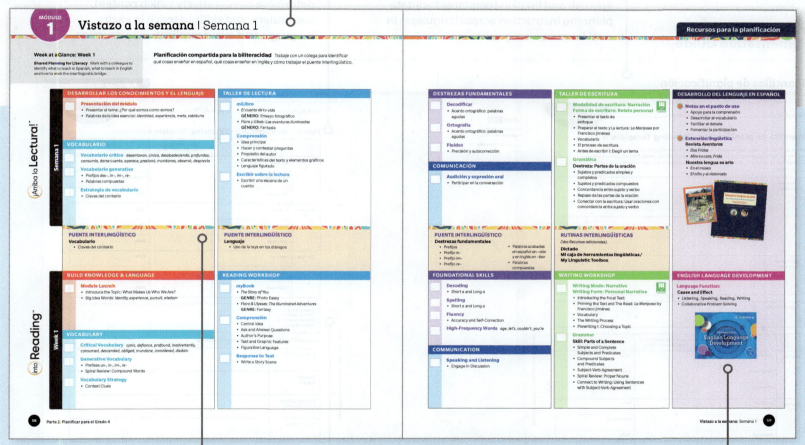

LANGUAGE BRIDGING
Determine the cross-linguistic instruction to use at "bridging" time.

DIFFERENTIATED INSTRUCTION
Target instruction for language learners with Spanish Language Development and English Language Development supports.

¡Arriba la Lectura! 139

Dual Language Program Planning

PART 3

The **Additional Resources** appendix includes **templates**, **rubrics**, and **instructional routines** to support dual language teaching and learning.

PLANNING TEMPLATES
Spanish and English templates facilitate planning instruction across languages in dual language programs.

PARTNER TEACHERS
Co-teachers can share templates to determine cooperatively which content, vocabulary, and skills to teach in each language and avoid duplicative instruction.

Dual Language Implementation Guide

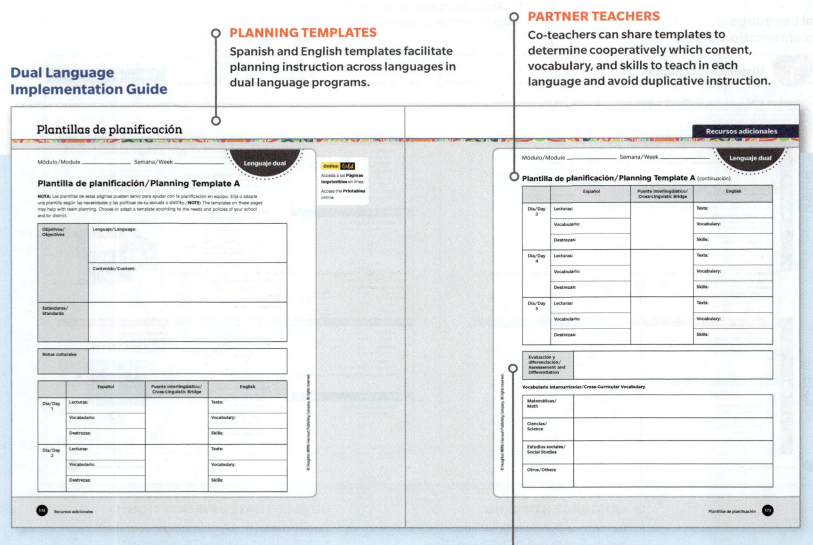

PARTNER TEACHERS
Work together to select the focus of each cross-linguistic bridge and to determine which tools to use for assessment and differentiation in each language.

¡ARRIBA LA LECTURA!

Dual Language Implementation Guide

RUBRICS
Biliteracy scoring rubrics offer partner language teachers a side-by-side view of individual children's growth in the four language domains and individual progress on the bilingual trajectory.

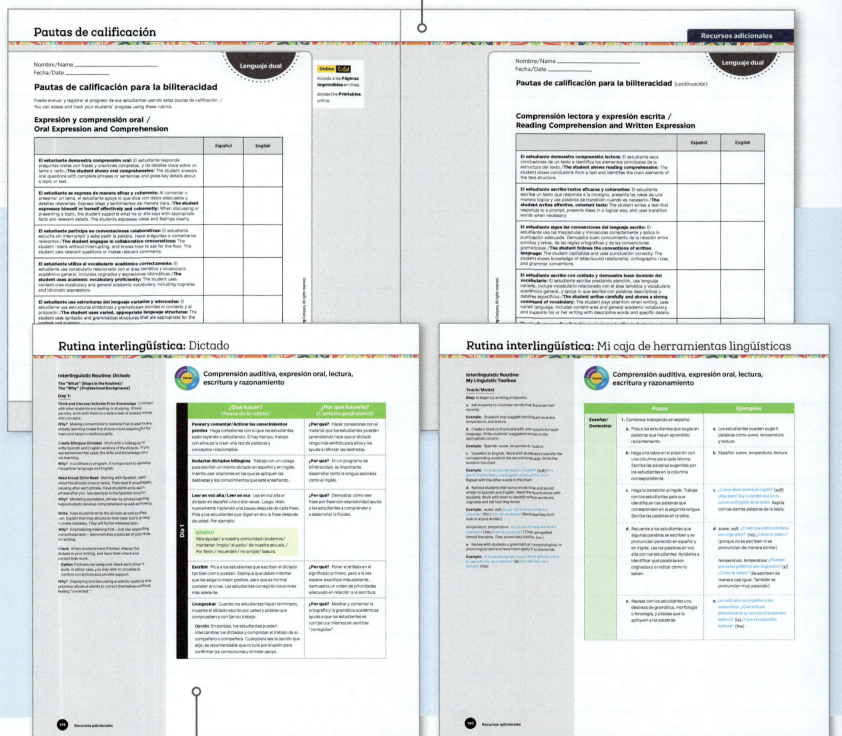

ROUTINES
Stepped-out cross-linguistic routines offer support for developing metalanguage in all learners, for implementing the *dictado,* and for imparting student-centered instruction in contrastive analysis.

¡Arriba la Lectura! 141

Notes

Literature Resources

Literature Resources

Module Topics and Text Sets 144
Text Complexity 152
Notice & Note 156
Rigby® Leveled Library 160

Literature Resources

Module Topics and Text Sets

Grade 1

	1 Nice to Meet You!	**2** My Family, My Community	**3** Amazing Animals
ESSENTIAL QUESTION	How can making new friends and learning new things help us?	How does everyone in my family and community make them special?	How do animals' bodies help them?
CROSS-CURRICULAR CONNECTION	New Friends and Experiences	Communities	How Animals Live
SOCIAL AND EMOTIONAL LEARNING	Relationship Skills	Social Awareness	Self-Awareness
TEXT SETS See the *¡Arriba la Lectura!* section for a complete list of culturally relevant and authentic texts.	**WEEK 1** • First Day Friends • My First Day • Pete the Cat: Rocking in My School Shoes • Try This! • Ralph Tells a Story **WEEK 2** • You Will Be My Friend! • My School Trip • A Kids' Guide to Friends **WEEK 3** • Suki's Kimono • Big Dilly's Tale • I'm Me	**WEEK 1** • Come to the Fair! • Kids Speak Up! • Whose Hands Are These? • Dan Had a Plan • Nana in the City **WEEK 2** • Maybe Something Beautiful • On the Map! • Places in My Neighborhood **WEEK 3** • Abuela • Who Put the Cookies in the Cookie Jar? • Curious About Jobs	**WEEK 1** • Hidden Animals • Animal Q & A • Best Foot Forward • The Nest • Giraffes **WEEK 2** • Whose Eye Am I? • Blue Bird and Coyote • Have You Heard the Nesting Bird? **WEEK 3** • Ol' Mama Squirrel • Step-by-Step Advice from the Animal Kingdom • Beaver Family
WRITING TYPE	Oral Story	Descriptive Essay	Research Essay

LITERATURE RESOURCES

 SOCIAL STUDIES   SCIENCE

4 Better Together	5 Now You See It, Now You Don't	6 Celebrate America
Why is it important to do my best and get along with others?	Why do light and dark come and go?	What do holidays and symbols tell about our country?
Being Good Citizens	Light and Dark	Holidays and Symbols
Relationship Skills	Responsible Decision-Making	Self-Awareness
WEEK 1 • Kindness Rewards • Good Sports • Baseball Hour • Goal! • Do Unto Otters **WEEK 2** • Pelé, King of Soccer • Get Up and Go! • Brontorina **WEEK 3** • The Great Ball Game • If You Plant a Seed • Color Your World with Kindness	**WEEK 1** • Light and Dark Together • Super Shadows! • On Earth • The Black Rabbit • Why the Sun and the Moon Live in the Sky **WEEK 2** • How Do You Know It's Winter? • Day and Night • The Best Season **WEEK 3** • Oscar and the Moth • What Are You Waiting For? • I'm So Hot	**WEEK 1** • America's Birthday • State the Facts! • You're a Grand Old Flag • Monument City • The Thanksgiving Door **WEEK 2** • Presidents' Day • The Contest • The Statue of Liberty **WEEK 3** • Can We Ring the Liberty Bell? • Hooray for Holidays! • Patriotic Poems
Procedural Text	Imaginative Story	Personal Narrative

Literature Resources

Module Topics and Text Sets

Grade 1

	7 The Big Outdoors	**8** Tell Me a Story	**9** Grow, Plants, Grow!
ESSENTIAL QUESTION	How do things in nature change?	What lessons can we learn from stories?	What do plants need to live and grow?
CROSS-CURRICULAR CONNECTION	The Natural World	What Stories Teach Us	Plants and Gardens
SOCIAL AND EMOTIONAL LEARNING	Social Awareness	Self-Management	Self-Management
TEXT SETS *See the ¡Arriba la Lectura! section for a complete list of culturally relevant and authentic texts.*	**WEEK 1** • Water in the Desert • Storm Report • Rainy, Sunny, Blowy, Snowy • Sam & Dave Dig a Hole • Ask Me **WEEK 2** • On Meadowview Street • Deserts • Handmade **WEEK 3** • Do You Really Want to Visit a Wetland? • Grand Canyon • Water Cycle	**WEEK 1** • The Mouse and the Lion • Follow the Story Path • Chicken Little • Interrupting Chicken • The Kissing Hand **WEEK 2** • Red Knit Cap Girl and the Reading Tree • Little Red Riding Hood • The Grasshopper & the Ants **WEEK 3** • My Name is Gabriela • Thank You, Mr. Aesop • The Tortoise and the Hare	**WEEK 1** • A Seed Grows • Plant Pairs • If I Were A Tree • So You Want to Grow a Taco? • One Bean **WEEK 2** • The Curious Garden • Which Part Do We Eat? • The Talking Vegetables **WEEK 3** • Amazing Plant Bodies • Yum! ¡MmMm! ¡Qué rico!: Americas' Sproutings • A Year in the Garden
WRITING TYPE	Poem	Personal Narrative	Descriptive Essay

LITERATURE RESOURCES

 SOCIAL STUDIES SCIENCE

10 Dare to Dream	11 Genre Study: Nonfiction	12 Genre Study: Literary Texts
How can thinking in new ways help solve problems?	What are the characteristics of narrative nonfiction, informational texts, and biography?	What are the characteristics of realistic fiction, folktales, and fantasy?
Thinking in New Ways	**WEEK 1** Narrative Nonfiction **WEEK 2** Informational Text **WEEK 3** Biography	**WEEK 1** Realistic Fiction **WEEK 2** Folktale **WEEK 3** Fantasy
Self-Management	Self-Awareness	Responsible Decision-Making
WEEK 1 • Reach for the Stars • Kids Are Inventors, Too! • What Can You Do? • Young Frank Architect • The Girl Who Could Dance in Outer Space **WEEK 2** • Charlotte the Scientist Is Squished • Sky Color • We Are the Future **WEEK 3** • I am Amelia Earhart • Joaquín's Zoo • Marconi and the Radio	**WEEK 1** • Try This! • Have You Heard the Nesting Bird? • Oscar and the Moth • Do You Really Want to Visit a Wetland? • Can We Ring the Liberty Bell? • I Will Not Read This Book **WEEK 2** • Animal Q & A • Amazing Plant Bodies • Whose Eye Am I? • Grand Canyon • Goal! **WEEK 3** • I am Amelia Earhart • Pelé, King of Soccer • My Name is Gabriela	**WEEK 1** • The Nest • Suki's Kimono • Maybe Something Beautiful • Sky Color • My School Trip • Big Bad Bubble **WEEK 2** • Chicken Little • Blue Bird and Coyote • The Talking Vegetables • The Great Ball Game **WEEK 3** • Ol' Mama Squirrel • Interrupting Chicken • Sam & Dave Dig a Hole • Brontorina • Red Knit Cap Girl and the Reading Tree
Biographical Essay	Opinion Letter	Opinion Essay

Literature Resources 147

Module Topics and Text Sets

Grade 2

	1 Be a Super Citizen	**2** Look Around and Explore!	**3** Meet in the Middle
ESSENTIAL QUESTION	How can being a good citizen make a difference to others?	How does exploring help us understand the world around us?	How can people work out disagreements?
CROSS-CURRICULAR CONNECTION	Citizenship	Discovering Our World	Solving Problems
SOCIAL AND EMOTIONAL LEARNING	Social Awareness	Self-Awareness	Relationship Skills
TEXT SETS See the *¡Arriba la Lectura!* section for a complete list of culturally relevant and authentic texts.	**WEEK 1** • Super Citizen • We Are Super Citizens • Meet the Dogs of Bedlam Farm • Clark the Shark • Just a Dream **WEEK 2** • The William Hoy Story • The Great Puppy Invasion • Being a Good Citizen **WEEK 3** • Violet the Pilot • Picture Day Perfection • Get Involved: Be Awesome!	**WEEK 1** • Mystery Animal Hunt • What's the Matter? • The Important Book • Many Kinds of Matter • Uncommon Traveler **WEEK 2** • It's Only Stanley • The Great Fuzz Frenzy • Water Rolls, Water Rises **WEEK 3** • If You Find a Rock • The Puddle Puzzle • Looking at Art	**WEEK 1** • The Compromise Kid • Meet Me Halfway • Mango, Abuela, and Me • Big Red Lollipop • Mr. Tiger Goes Wild **WEEK 2** • Three Hens and a Peacock • Working with Others • Gingerbread for Liberty! **WEEK 3** • Serious Farm • Pepita and the Bully • Be a Hero! Work It Out!
WRITING TYPE	Personal Narrative	Descriptive Essay	Persuasive Text

LITERATURE RESOURCES

 SOCIAL STUDIES   SCIENCE

4 Once Upon a Time

What lessons can we learn from the characters in stories?

Storytelling

Self-Awareness

WEEK 1
- Ever After
- Recipe for a Fairy Tale
- Goldilocks and the Three Dinosaurs
- How to Read a Story
- Aunt Isabel Tells a Good One

WEEK 2
- Rabbit's Snow Dance
- A Crow, a Lion, and a Mouse! Oh, My!
- Hollywood Chicken

WEEK 3
- A Perfect Season for Dreaming
- If the Shoe Fits: Two Cinderella Stories
- Those Clever Crows

Imaginative Story

5 Lead the Way

What are the qualities of a good leader?

Leadership

Self-Management

WEEK 1
- What It Takes to Be a Great Leader
- What's Good to Read? Book Reviews for Kids by Kids!
- Seed by Seed: The Legend and Legacy of John "Appleseed" Chapman
- Going Places
- Stand Tall, Molly Lou Melon

WEEK 2
- My Dream Playground
- Wilma Rudolph: Against All Odds
- Great Leaders

WEEK 3
- Whoosh!: Lonnie Johnson's Super-Soaking Stream of Inventions
- Who Are Government's Leaders?
- Thomas Edison and the Light Bulb

Personal Essay

6 Weather Wise

How does the weather affect us?

Weather

Social Awareness

WEEK 1
- Wonderful Weather!
- Weather Through the Seasons
- Freddy the Frogcaster
- Wild Weather
- When the Moon Is Full: A Lunar Year

WEEK 2
- The Story of Snow: The Science of Winter's Wonder
- Cloudette
- Get Ready for Weather

WEEK 3
- Fall Leaves
- Whatever the Weather
- Rain Cloud in a Jar

Poem

Module Topics and Text Sets

Grade 2

	7 Everyone Has a Story	**8** Time to Grow!	**9** Home Sweet Habitat
ESSENTIAL QUESTION	How do our experiences shape our lives?	What do plants need to live and grow?	How do living things in a habitat depend on each other?
CROSS-CURRICULAR CONNECTION	Important People	Plants	Animal Habitats
SOCIAL AND EMOTIONAL LEARNING	Self-Management	Self-Management	Relationship Skills
TEXT SETS See the *¡Arriba la Lectura!* section for a complete list of culturally relevant and authentic texts.	**WEEK 1** • The Story of Me • Get to Know Biographies • Miss Moore Thought Otherwise • I Am Helen Keller • How I Became a Pirate **WEEK 2** • The Camping Trip That Changed America: Theodore Roosevelt, John Muir, and Our National Parks • How to Make a Timeline • The Stories He Tells: The Story of Joseph Bruchac **WEEK 3** • Molly, by Golly! • Drum Dream Girl • Roberto Clemente	**WEEK 1** • Totally Growing Live • The Growth of a Sunflower • From Seed to Pine Tree: Following the Life Cycle • Experiment with What a Plant Needs to Grow • From Seed to Plant **WEEK 2** • The Legend of the Indian Paintbrush • Jack and the Beanstalk • Jackie and the Beanstalk **WEEK 3** • The Patchwork Garden • Don't Touch Me! • George Washington Carver: The Wizard of Tuskegee	**WEEK 1** • Creature Comforts • The Best Habitat for Me • Nature's Patchwork Quilt: Understanding Habitats • The Long, Long Journey • The Great Kapok Tree **WEEK 2** • Kali's Story: An Orphaned Polar Bear Rescue • Sea Otter Pups • At Home in the Wild **WEEK 3** • Out of the Woods: A True Story of an Unforgettable Event • Abuelo and the Three Bears • Ducklings Jump from Nest
WRITING TYPE	Imaginative Story	Procedural Text	Research Report

LITERATURE RESOURCES

 SOCIAL STUDIES SCIENCE

10 Many Cultures, One World	11 Genre Study: Nonfiction	12 Genre Study: Literary Texts
What can we learn from different people and cultures?	What are the characteristics of biography, opinion writing, and informational texts?	What are the characteristics of realistic fiction, fantasy, and poetry?
World Cultures	WEEK 1 Biography WEEK 2 Opinion Writing WEEK 3 Informational Text	WEEK 1 Realistic Fiction WEEK 2 Fantasy WEEK 3 Poetry
Social Awareness	Responsible Decision-Making	Responsible Decision-Making
WEEK 1 • Fiesta! • Hello, World! • Trombone Shorty • Where on Earth Is My Bagel? • The Name Jar **WEEK 2** • Time for Cranberries • May Day Around the World • Goal! **WEEK 3** • Dreams Around the World • Poems in the Attic • What's for Lunch Around the World?	**WEEK 1** • I Am Helen Keller • Gingerbread for Liberty! • Trombone Shorty • The Stories He Tells: The Story of Joseph Bruchac • Wilma Rudolph: Against All Odds • Roller Coaster **WEEK 2** • Great Leaders • Get to Know Biographies • The Best Habitat for Me • What's Good to Read? Book Reviews for Kids by Kids! **WEEK 3** • Sea Otter Pups • Many Kinds of Matter • Get Ready for Weather • How to Read a Story • Experiment with What a Plant Needs to Grow	**WEEK 1** • Big Red Lollipop • Where on Earth Is My Bagel? • Pepita and the Bully • Picture Day Perfection • My Dream Playground • The Dot **WEEK 2** • Clark the Shark • Three Hens and a Peacock • Hollywood Chicken • The Great Puppy Invasion • The Great Fuzz Frenzy **WEEK 3** • At Home in the Wild • Whatever the Weather • Water Rolls, Water Rises • Drum Dream Girl • Poems in the Attic
Thank-You Letter	Personal Narrative	Opinion Essay

Text Complexity

Use this table as a reference for the text complexity measures of the Grade 1 *my*Book texts.

Grade 1 *my*Book

	Title	Author	Genre	Lexile	Guided Reading Level	Qualitative Measure
M1	My First Day		Realistic Fiction	150L	E	Simple
	Try This!	Pam Muñoz Ryan	Narrative Nonfiction	60L	D	Simple
	My School Trip	Aly G. Mays	Realistic Fiction	140L	E	Simple
	A Kids' Guide to Friends	Trey Amico	Informational Text	230L	F	Slightly Complex
	Big Dilly's Tale	Gail Carson Levine	Fairy Tale	360L	F	Moderately Complex
M2	Kids Speak Up!		Opinion Writing	210L	D	Slightly Complex
	Dan Had a Plan	Wong Herbert Yee	Realistic Fiction	250L	E	Slightly Complex
	On the Map!	Lisa Fleming	Informational Text	240L	C	Simple
	Places in My Neighborhood	Shelly Lyons	Informational Text	IG470L	I	Moderately Complex
	Who Put the Cookies in the Cookie Jar?	George Shannon	Informational Text	420L	G	Moderately Complex
M3	Animal Q & A		Informational Text	310L	E	Slightly Complex
	The Nest	Carole Roberts	Realistic Fiction	260L	F	Slightly Complex
	Blue Bird and Coyote	James Bruchac	Folktale	310L	F	Slightly Complex
	Have You Heard the Nesting Bird?	Rita Gray	Narrative Nonfiction	AD430L	G	Moderately Complex
	Step-by-Step Advice from the Animal Kingdom	Steve Jenkins and Robin Page	Procedural Text	480L	H	Moderately Complex
M4	Good Sports		Opinion Writing	380L	G	Slightly Complex
	Goal!	Jane Medina	Informational Text	480L	H	Moderately Complex
	Get Up and Go!	Rozanne Lanczak Williams	Informational Text	370L	F	Slightly Complex
	Brontorina	James Howe	Fantasy	470L	L	Slightly Complex
	If You Plant a Seed	Kadir Nelson	Fantasy	AD340L	G	Moderately Complex
M5	Super Shadows!		Informational Text	290L	G	Slightly Complex
	The Black Rabbit	Philippa Leathers	Fantasy	470L	K	Moderately Complex
	Day and Night	Margaret Hall	Informational Text	390L	J	Slightly Complex
	The Best Season	Nina Crews	Opinion Writing	400L	I	Slightly Complex
	What Are You Waiting For?	Scott Menchin	Fantasy	250L	F	Simple

LITERATURE RESOURCES

Grade 1 myBook continued

	Title	Author	Genre	Lexile	Guided Reading Level	Qualitative Measure
M6	State the Facts!		Informational Text	360L	H	Simple
	Monument City	Jerdine Nolen	Drama	NP	L	Moderately Complex
	The Contest	Libby Martinez	Opinion Writing	490L	J	Moderately Complex
	The Statue of Liberty	Tyler Monroe	Informational Text	550L	N	Very Complex
	Hooray for Holidays!	Pat Cummings	Realistic Fiction	450L	K	Slightly Complex
	Patriotic Poems	various poets	Poetry	NP	K	Moderately Complex
M7	Storm Report		Opinion Writing	430L	I	Moderately Complex
	Sam & Dave Dig a Hole	Mac Barnett	Fantasy	450L	L	Moderately Complex
	Deserts	Quinn M. Arnold	Informational Text	300L	H	Slightly Complex
	Handmade	Guadalupe Rodríguez	Procedural Text	470L	K	Moderately Complex
	Grand Canyon	Sara Gilbert	Informational Text	480L	H	Moderately Complex
M8	Follow the Story Path		Informational Text	490L	H	Slightly Complex
	Interrupting Chicken	David Ezra Stein	Fantasy	AD510L	L	Very Complex
	Little Red Riding Hood	Lisa Campbell Ernst	Drama	NP	K	Moderately Complex
	The Grasshopper & the Ants	Jerry Pinkney	Fable	470L	K	Moderately Complex
	Thank You, Mr. Aesop	Helen Lester	Informational Text	520L	M	Very Complex
M9	Plant Pairs		Poetry	NP	K	Very Complex
	So You Want to Grow a Taco?	Bridget Heos	Procedural Text	510L	L	Moderately Complex
	Which Part Do We Eat?	Katherine Ayres	Poetry	NP	K	Slightly Complex
	The Talking Vegetables	Won-Ldy Paye and Margaret H. Lippert	Folktale	550L	K	Very Complex
	Yum! ¡MmMm! ¡Qué rico!	Pat Mora	Poetry	NP	L	Moderately Complex
M10	Kids Are Inventors, Too!		Informational Text	490L	J	Slightly Complex
	Young Frank Architect	Frank Viva	Realistic Fiction	500L	K	Moderately Complex
	Sky Color	Peter H. Reynolds	Realistic Fiction	AD550L	K	Very Complex
	We Are the Future	various poets	Poetry	NP	J	Moderately Complex
	Joaquín's Zoo	Pablo Bernasconi	Fantasy	580L	K	Very Complex

Text Complexity

Use this table as a reference for the text complexity measures of the Grade 2 *my*Book texts.

Grade 2 *my*Book

	Title	Author	Genre	Lexile	Guided Reading Level	Qualitative Measure
M1	We Are Super Citizens		Personal Narrative	530L	K	Slightly Complex
	Clark the Shark	Bruce Hale	Fantasy	500L	M	Slightly Complex
	The Great Puppy Invasion	Alastair Heim	Fantasy	520L	L	Slightly Complex
	Being a Good Citizen	Rachelle Kreisman	Informational Text	530L	N	Moderately Complex
	Picture Day Perfection	Deborah Diesen	Realistic Fiction	570L	M	Moderately Complex
M2	What's the Matter?		Informational Text	440L	L	Moderately Complex
	Many Kinds of Matter	Jennifer Boothroyd	Informational Text	530L	M	Moderately Complex
	The Great Fuzz Frenzy	Janet Stevens and Susan Stevens Crummel	Fantasy	420L	K	Slightly Complex
	Water Rolls, Water Rises	Pat Mora	Poetry	NP	P	Moderately Complex
	The Puddle Puzzle	Ellen Weiss	Drama	NP	L	Slightly Complex
	Looking at Art	Andrew Stevens	Fine Art	630L	M	Moderately Complex
M3	Meet Me Halfway		Informational Text	450L	K	Very Complex
	Big Red Lollipop	Rukhsana Khan	Realistic Fiction	490L	M	Moderately Complex
	Working with Others	Robin Nelson	Informational Text	490L	L	Slightly Complex
	Gingerbread for Liberty!	Mara Rockliff	Biography	590L	M	Moderately Complex
	Pepita and the Bully	Ofelia Dumas Lachtman	Realistic Fiction	530L	L	Slightly Complex
	Be a Hero! Work It Out!	Ruben Cooley	Infographic	530L	L	Moderately Complex
M4	Recipe for a Fairy Tale		Recipe	490L	K	Moderately Complex
	How to Read a Story	Kate Messner	Procedural Text	480L	L	Slightly Complex
	A Crow, a Lion, and a Mouse! Oh, My!	Crystal Hubbard	Drama	NP	K	Moderately Complex
	Hollywood Chicken	Lisa Fleming	Fantasy	600L	L	Very Complex
	If the Shoe Fits: Two Cinderella Stories	Pleasant DeSpain	Fairy Tales	580L	M	Moderately Complex
M5	What's Good to Read? Book Reviews for Kids by Kids!		Opinion Article	690L	L	Moderately Complex
	Going Places	Peter and Paul Reynolds	Fantasy	480L	M	Moderately Complex
	Wilma Rudolph: Against All Odds	Stephanie E. Macceca	Biography	570L	N	Moderately Complex
	Great Leaders		Opinion Writing	520L	N	Moderately Complex
	Who Are Government's Leaders?	Jennifer Boothroyd	Informational Text	580L	L	Moderately Complex

LITERATURE RESOURCES

Grade 2 myBook continued

	Title	Author	Genre	Lexile	Guided Reading Level	Qualitative Measure
M6	Weather Through the Seasons		Informational Text	500L	L	Very Complex
	Wild Weather	Thomas Kingsley Troupe	Narrative Nonfiction	590L	O	Very Complex
	Cloudette	Tom Lichtenheld	Fantasy	590L	K	Moderately Complex
	Get Ready for Weather	Lucy Jones	Informational Text	580L	L	Moderately Complex
	Whatever the Weather	various poets	Poetry	NP	K	Moderately Complex
M7	Get to Know Biographies		Opinion Essay	560L	L	Moderately Complex
	I Am Helen Keller	Brad Meltzer	Biography	560L	O	Very Complex
	How to Make a Timeline	Boyd N. Gillin	Procedural Text	530L	L	Moderately Complex
	The Stories He Tells: The Story of Joseph Bruchac	James Bruchac	Biography	700L	M	Moderately Complex
	Drum Dream Girl	Margarita Engle	Poetry	NP	L	Very Complex
M8	The Growth of a Sunflower		Photo Essay	490L	J	Moderately Complex
	Experiment with What a Plant Needs to Grow	Nadia Higgins	Informational Text	570L	M	Moderately Complex
	Jack and the Beanstalk	Helen Lester	Fairy Tale	550L	M	Moderately Complex
	Jackie and the Beanstalk	Lori Mortensen	Fairy Tale	660L	M	Very Complex
	Don't Touch Me!	Elizabeth Preston	Informational Text	600L	M	Moderately Complex
M9	The Best Habitat for Me		Opinion Essay	620L	L	Moderately Complex
	The Long, Long Journey	Sandra Markle	Informational Text	610L	M	Very Complex
	Sea Otter Pups	Ruth Owen	Informational Text	600L	I	Moderately Complex
	At Home in the Wild	various poets	Poetry	NP	L	Moderately Complex
	Abuelo and the Three Bears	Jerry Tello	Folktale	460L	L	Moderately Complex
M10	Hello, World!		Informational Text	540L	M	Moderately Complex
	Where on Earth Is My Bagel?	Frances and Ginger Park	Realistic Fiction	590L	L	Moderately Complex
	May Day Around the World	Tori Telfer	Narrative Nonfiction	600L	L	Moderately Complex
	Goal!	Sean Taylor	Informational Text	620L	M	Moderately Complex
	Poems in the Attic	Nikki Grimes	Poetry	NP	N	Very Complex

Literature Resources 155

Notice & Note

Use the Notice & Note Signposts for fiction and nonfiction to support close reading.

Notice & Note Signposts at a Glance

Fiction		Nonfiction	
Contrasts and Contradictions	Again and Again	Contrasts and Contradictions	Quoted Words
Words of the Wiser	Memory Moment	Extreme or Absolute Language	Word Gaps
Aha Moment	Tough Questions	Numbers and Stats	3 Big Questions

Teacher's Guide

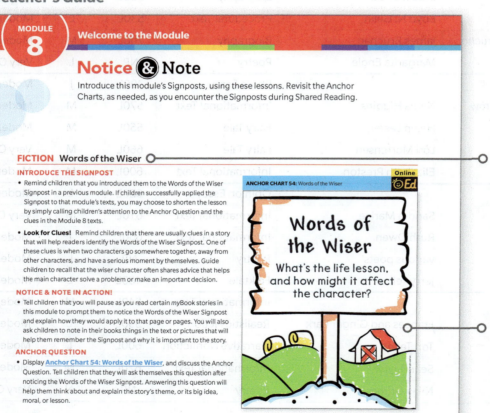

INTRODUCE THE SIGNPOST
Introduce the focus fiction and nonfiction **Notice & Note Signposts** for each module, using the lesson in the Teacher's Guide module overview pages.

USE AN ANCHOR CHART
Display and return to the Notice & Note **Anchor Charts** throughout the module to remind children of each Signpost's **Anchor Question**.

APPLY TO LITERATURE
Note the texts in each module that feature the focus Signposts in the **Teaching Pal**.

156 Program Guide • Grades 1–2

Use this table as a reference for where the Notice & Note Signposts appear with **fiction** texts.

Grade 1 Fiction

	Lesson	myBook Texts	Genre	Signpost
M1	7	My School Trip	Realistic Fiction	Contrasts and Contradictions
	12	Big Dilly's Tale	Fairy Tale	Contrasts and Contradictions
M2	3	Dan Had a Plan	Realistic Fiction	Aha Moment
M3	3	The Nest	Realistic Fiction	Again and Again
	7	Blue Bird and Coyote	Folktale	Again and Again
M4	9	Brontorina	Fantasy	Aha Moment
	12	If You Plant a Seed	Fantasy	Aha Moment
M5	3	The Black Rabbit	Fantasy	Aha Moment
	12	What Are You Waiting For?	Fantasy	Aha Moment
M6	3	Monument City	Drama	Words of the Wiser
	12	Hooray for Holidays!	Realistic Fiction	Words of the Wiser
M7	3	Sam & Dave Dig a Hole	Fantasy	Again and Again
M8	3	Interrupting Chicken	Fantasy	Words of the Wiser
	7	Little Red Riding Hood	Drama	Words of the Wiser
	9	The Grasshopper & the Ants	Fable	Words of the Wiser
M9	7	Which Part Do We Eat?	Poetry	Again and Again
	9	The Talking Vegetables	Folktale	Again and Again
M10	3	Young Frank Architect	Realistic Fiction	Contrasts and Contradictions
	7	Sky Color	Realistic Fiction	Contrasts and Contradictions
	12	Joaquin's Zoo	Fantasy	Contrasts and Contradictions

Grade 2 Fiction

	Lesson	myBook Texts	Genre	Signpost
M1	3	Clark the Shark	Fantasy	Words of the Wiser
M2	2	The Great Fuzz Frenzy	Fantasy	Aha Moment
	3	The Puddle Puzzle	Drama	Aha Moment
M3	3	Big Red Lollipop	Realistic Fiction	Contrasts and Contradictions
	12	Pepita and the Bully	Realistic Fiction	Contrasts and Contradictions
M4	7	A Crow, a Lion, and a Mouse! Oh, My!	Drama	Again and Again
	9	Hollywood Chicken	Fantasy	Again and Again
	12	If the Shoe Fits: Two Cinderella Stories	Fairy Tales	Again and Again
M5	3	Going Places	Fantasy	Tough Questions
M6	7	Cloudette	Fantasy	Aha Moment

Literature Resources

Notice & Note Signposts

Grade 2 Fiction continued

	Lesson	myBook Texts	Genre	Signpost
M7	12	Drum Dream Girl	Poetry	Again and Again
M8	7	Jack and the Beanstalk	Fairy Tale	Contrasts and Contradictions
	9	Jackie and the Beanstalk	Fairy Tale	Contrasts and Contradictions
M9	12	Abuelo and the Three Bears	Folktale	Memory Moment
M10	3	Where on Earth Is My Bagel?	Realistic Fiction	Again and Again
	12	Poems in the Attic	Poetry	Again and Again

Use this table as a reference for where the Notice & Note Signposts appear with nonfiction texts.

Grade 1 Nonfiction

	Lesson	myBook Texts	Genre	Signpost
M1	3	Try This!	Narrative Nonfiction	3 Big Questions
	9	A Kids' Guide to Friends	Informational Text	3 Big Questions
M2	7	On the Map!	Informational Text	3 Big Questions
	9	Places in My Neighborhood	Informational Text	3 Big Questions
	12	Who Put the Cookies in the Cookie Jar?	Informational Text	3 Big Questions
M3	9	Have You Heard the Nesting Bird?	Narrative Nonfiction	Contrasts and Contradictions
	12	Step-by-Step Advice from the Animal Kingdom	Procedural Text	Contrasts and Contradictions
M4	3	Goal!	Informational Text	Word Gaps
	7	Get Up and Go!	Informational Text	Word Gaps
M5	7	Day and Night	Informational Text	Contrasts and Contradictions
	9	The Best Season	Opinion Writing	Contrasts and Contradictions
M6	7	The Contest	Opinion Writing	Numbers and Stats
	9	The Statue of Liberty	Informational Text	Numbers and Stats
M7	7	Deserts	Informational Text	Numbers and Stats
	9	Handmade	Procedural Text	Numbers and Stats
	12	Grand Canyon	Informational Text	Numbers and Stats
M8	12	Thank You, Mr. Aesop	Informational Text	Contrasts and Contradictions
M9	3	So You Want to Grow a Taco?	Procedural Text	Word Gaps

LITERATURE RESOURCES

Grade 2 Nonfiction

	Lesson	myBook Texts	Genre	Signpost
M1	9	Being a Good Citizen	Informational Text	3 Big Questions
M2	1	Many Kinds of Matter	Informational Text	Contrasts and Contradictions
M3	7	Working with Others	Informational Text	Extreme or Absolute Language
	9	Gingerbread for Liberty!	Biography	Extreme or Absolute Language
	14	Be a Hero! Work It Out!	Infographic	Extreme or Absolute Language
M4	3	How to Read a Story	Procedural Text	Quoted Words
M5	7	Wilma Rudolph: Against All Odds	Biography	Contrasts and Contradictions
	9	Great Leaders	Opinion Writing	Contrasts and Contradictions
	12	Who Are Government's Leaders?	Informational Text	Contrasts and Contradictions
M6	3	Wild Weather	Narrative Nonfiction	Numbers and Stats
	12	Get Ready for Weather	Informational Text	Numbers and Stats
M7	3	I Am Helen Keller	Biography	Contrasts and Contradictions
	7	How to Make a Timeline	Procedural Text	Contrasts and Contradictions
	9	The Stories He Tells: The Story of Joseph Bruchac	Biography	Contrasts and Contradictions
M8	3	Experiment with What a Plant Needs to Grow	Informational Text	Word Gaps
	12	Don't Touch Me!	Informational Text	Word Gaps
M9	3	The Long, Long Journey	Informational Text	Numbers and Stats
	7	Sea Otter Pups	Informational Text	Numbers and Stats
M10	7	May Day Around the World	Narrative Nonfiction	Contrasts and Contradictions
	9	Goal!	Informational Text	Contrasts and Contradictions

Literature Resources 159

Rigby Leveled Library

Grade 1

Title	Genre	Guided Reading Level	Lexile	Take & Teach Instructional Sessions		
Boss Is Hungry	Realistic Fiction	C	140L	Key Ideas and Details	Characters	Story Structure
Grandpa	Realistic Fiction	C	150L	Key Ideas and Details	Characters	Point of View
Helping Each Other	Realistic Fiction	C	140L	Key Ideas and Details	Characters	Setting
Little Cat and Big Cat	Animal Fantasy	C	150L	Key Ideas and Details	Characters	Story Structure
Now It's Hot!	Informational Text	C	10L	Key Ideas and Details	Central Idea	Text Organization
Play Ball!	Informational Text	C	200L	Key Ideas and Details	Central Idea	Text Organization
The Five Senses	Informational Text	C	100L	Key Ideas and Details	Author's Purpose	Text Features
Tick, Tock, Check the Clock!	Animal Fantasy	C	140L	Key Ideas and Details	Setting	Story Structure
What Is Hiding?	Informational Text	C	110L	Key Ideas and Details	Content-Area Words	Text Organization
Who Is Hungry?	Informational Text	C	160L	Key Ideas and Details	Central Idea	Content-Area Words
Animal Shapes	Informational Text	D	370L	Key Ideas and Details	Content-Area Words	Text Organization
Little Squirrel Wants to Play	Animal Fantasy	D	300L	Key Ideas and Details	Setting	Theme
Little Terriers	Informational Text	D	170L	Key Ideas and Details	Author's Purpose	Text Features
Lizard Loses His Tail	Realistic Fiction	D	170L	Key Ideas and Details	Chronological Order	Author's Purpose
Our Flag	Informational Text	D	130L	Key Ideas and Details	Central Idea	Text Organization
Our Gift to the Beach	Informational Text	D	150L	Key Ideas and Details	Central Idea	Chronological Order
Playing in the Snow	Informational Text/ Letter	D	160L	Key Ideas and Details	Chronological Order	Point of View
The Hungry Kitten	Animal Fantasy	D	200L	Key Ideas and Details	Characters	Point of View
The Little Green Car	Realistic Fiction	D	240L	Key Ideas and Details	Characters	Story Structure
This Is My Family	Realistic Fiction	D	190L	Key Ideas and Details	Characters	Point of View
Buddy's Bath	Realistic Fiction	E	240L	Key Ideas and Details	Chronological Order	Story Structure
Cold Day, Hot Chocolate	Realistic Fiction	E	240L	Key Ideas and Details	Setting	Story Structure
Everyone Says Sh-h-h-h!	Realistic Fiction	E	170L	Key Ideas and Details	Point of View	Theme
Fire! Fire!	Realistic Fiction	E	250L	Key Ideas and Details	Setting	Story Structure
Looking at Insects	Informational Text	E	160L	Key Ideas and Details	Content-Area Words	Text Features
Monarch Mystery	Mystery	E	380L	Key Ideas and Details	Author's Purpose	Point of View
My Vacation Diary	Informational Text/ Diary	E	300L	Key Ideas and Details	Chronological Order	Content-Area Words
Our Vegetable Garden	Informational Text	E	350L	Key Ideas and Details	Chronological Order	Ideas and Support
Planting and Growing	Procedural Text	E	310L	Key Ideas and Details	Content-Area Words	Point of View
Stay Safe!	Informational Text	E	310L	Key Ideas and Details	Author's Purpose	Central Idea
A Lucky Day for Little Dinosaur	Animal Fantasy	F	330L	Key Ideas and Details	Setting	Story Structure
Corn for Sale	Informational Text	F	360L	Key Ideas and Details	Central Idea	Text Features
July Fourth!	Informational Text	F	390L	Key Ideas and Details	Central Idea	Text Organization

LITERATURE RESOURCES

Grade 1 continued

Title	Genre	Guided Reading Level	Lexile	Take & Teach Instructional Sessions		
Our Garden Diary	Informational Text/Diary	F	320L	Key Ideas and Details	Chronological Order	Point of View
Stars in the Sky	Informational Text	F	330L	Key Ideas and Details	Text Features	Text Organization
The Children's Farm	Informational Text	F	320L	Key Ideas and Details	Point of View	Text Organization
The Little Ant and the White Bird	Fable	F	330L	Key Ideas and Details	Story Structure	Theme
The Monster in the Attic	Realistic Fiction	F	340L	Key Ideas and Details	Setting	Story Structure
The Saturday Cat	Realistic Fiction	F	410L	Key Ideas and Details	Characters	Story Structure
Who Needs Rooster?	Animal Fantasy	F	540L	Key Ideas and Details	Characters	Story Structure
Bigger	Informational Text	G	360L	Key Ideas and Details	Central Idea	Text Organization
Enter at Your Own Risk	Informational Text	G	400L	Key Ideas and Details	Text Organization	Text Features
How Do You Sleep?	Informational Text	G	380L	Key Ideas and Details	Author's Purpose	Central Idea
Mom Is Late	Realistic Fiction	G	320L	Key Ideas and Details	Characters	Point of View
Oh, Baby!	Informational Text	G	190L	Key Ideas and Details	Central Idea	Text Features
Rex Runs Away	Realistic Fiction	G	510L	Key Ideas and Details	Setting	Story Structure
Save Stan's Tree	Animal Fantasy	G	360L	Key Ideas and Details	Characters	Point of View
The Angry Bear	Fable	G	280L	Key Ideas and Details	Story Structure	Theme
The Donkey and the Wolf	Fable	G	340L	Key Ideas and Details	Characters	Theme
The Vet	Informational Text	G	360L	Key Ideas and Details	Content-Area Words	Point of View
Buddy	Realistic Fiction	H	450L	Key Ideas and Details	Characters	Setting
How Gliders Fly	Informational Text	H	420L	Key Ideas and Details	Author's Purpose	Ideas and Support
Marisol's Mystery	Mystery	H	450L	Key Ideas and Details	Setting	Story Structure
Secrets of the Seahorse	Informational Text	H	400L	Key Ideas and Details	Content-Area Words	Text Organization
Snowy Days	Informational Text	H	380L	Key Ideas and Details	Central Idea	Content-Area Words
Thanksgiving Day	Informational Text	H	450L	Key Ideas and Details	Author's Purpose	Central Idea
The Creek at the Farm	Realistic Fiction	H	470L	Key Ideas and Details	Characters	Story Structure
The Fox and the Stork	Fable	H	410L	Key Ideas and Details	Characters	Theme
Tomatoes Everywhere	Informational Text	H	440L	Key Ideas and Details	Author's Purpose	Central Idea
Tooth on the Loose	Realistic Fiction	H	450L	Key Ideas and Details	Characters	Chronological Order
Animals That Live Under the Ground	Informational Text	I	490L	Key Ideas and Details	Central Idea	Content-Area Words
Ants	Informational Text	I	430L	Key Ideas and Details	Content-Area Words	Text Features
Biggest, Smallest, Fastest, Slowest	Informational Text	I	470L	Key Ideas and Details	Central Idea	Text Features
Flying Jewels	Informational Text	I	390L	Key Ideas and Details	Text Features	Text Organization
On the Farm	Realistic Fiction	I	490L	Key Ideas and Details	Characters	Story Structure
Our Town	Informational Text	I	320L	Key Ideas and Details	Text Features	Text Organization
Read the Signs	Animal Fantasy	I	440L	Key Ideas and Details	Characters	Setting

Rigby Leveled Library

Grade 1 continued

Title	Genre	Guided Reading Level	Lexile	Take & Teach Instructional Sessions		
Rodeo Under the Sea	Animal Fantasy	I	520L	Key Ideas and Details	Characters	Story Structure
The Country School	Realistic Fiction	I	430L	Key Ideas and Details	Point of View	Setting
The Peacock and the Crane	Fable	I	440L	Key Ideas and Details	Story Structure	Theme
Apples for Sale!	Realistic Fiction	J	480L	Key Ideas and Details	Characters	Story Structure
Crabs	Informational Text	J	440L	Key Ideas and Details	Content-Area Words	Text Organization
Dad, the Bird Caller	Realistic Fiction	J	520L	Key Ideas and Details	Characters	Point of View
Don't Stomp on That Bug!	Informational Text	J	480L	Key Ideas and Details	Author's Purpose	Ideas and Support
Pulleys and Gears	Informational Text	J	550L	Key Ideas and Details	Content-Area Words	Text Features
Tarantulas!	Informational Text	J	490L	Key Ideas and Details	Central Idea	Content-Area Words
The Best Animal in the Forest	Drama/Fable	J	530L	Key Ideas and Details	Characters	Theme
The Mystery of the Missing Berries	Mystery	J	520L	Key Ideas and Details	Point of View	Story Structure
The Princess and the Pea	Fairy Tale	J	470L	Key Ideas and Details	Setting	Story Structure
Water Sports	Informational Text	J	530L	Key Ideas and Details	Author's Purpose	Central Idea
A Bundle of Sticks	Fable	K	510L	Key Ideas and Details	Story Structure	Theme
A New Friend	Realistic Fiction	K	550L	Key Ideas and Details	Characters	Theme
All About Bikes	Informational Text	K	530L	Key Ideas and Details	Author's Purpose	Content-Area Words
Honey	Informational Text/Letter	K	500L	Key Ideas and Details	Author's Purpose	Text Organization
Lizard on the Loose	Realistic Fiction	K	480L	Key Ideas and Details	Characters	Story Structure
Night Work	Informational Text	K	540L	Key Ideas and Details	Central Idea	Content-Area Words
Noises in the Night	Realistic Fiction	K	590L	Key Ideas and Details	Setting	Story Structure
Plants We Use	Informational Text	K	490L	Key Ideas and Details	Author's Purpose	Central Idea
The Emperor's New Clothes	Drama/Fairy Tale	K	550L	Key Ideas and Details	Characters	Theme
What Is Soil?	Informational Text	K	490L	Key Ideas and Details	Content-Area Words	Text Features

LITERATURE RESOURCES

Grade 2

Title	Genre	Guided Reading Level	Lexile	Take & Teach Instructional Sessions		
A Visit to the Butterfly House	Realistic Fiction	I	480L	Key Ideas and Details	Connect Text and Visuals	Point of View
Emperor Penguins	Informational Text	I	510L	Key Ideas and Details	Author's Purpose	Central Idea
Gardens	Realistic Fiction/Opinion Text	I	500L	Key Ideas and Details	Author's Purpose	Content-Area Words
How Living Things Help Each Other	Informational Text	I	420L	Key Ideas and Details	Central Idea	Text and Graphic Features
Is the Wise Owl Wise?	Animal Fantasy	I	510L	Key Ideas and Details	Theme	Setting
Little Dragon Boats	Realistic Fiction	I	510L	Key Ideas and Details	Author's Purpose	Connect Text and Visuals
Our Five Senses	Informational Text	I	380L	Key Ideas and Details	Central Idea	Author's Purpose
Pop's Old Car	Realistic Fiction	I	510L	Key Ideas and Details	Text Organization	Characters
Saving Scruffy	Realistic Fiction	I	410L	Key Ideas and Details	Characters	Story Structure
Special Days, Special Dances	Informational Text/Interview	I	530L	Key Ideas and Details	Central Idea	Author's Purpose
The Ant and the Dove	Fable	I	470L	Key Ideas and Details	Story Structure	Theme
The Mighty Mississippi	Informational Text	I	510L	Key Ideas and Details	Text and Graphic Features	Connect Text and Visuals
The Missing Bag	Realistic Fiction	I	460L	Key Ideas and Details	Point of View	Story Structure
The Troll Under the Bridge	Fairy Tale	I	490L	Key Ideas and Details	Setting	Characters
Windy Days	Informational Text	I	400L	Key Ideas and Details	Central Idea	Text Organization
A Dictionary of Snake Facts	Informational Text	J	500L	Key Ideas and Details	Text and Graphic Features	Author's Purpose
BMX Bikes	Informational Text	J	530L	Key Ideas and Details	Author's Purpose	Ideas and Support
Desert Life	Informational Text	J	470L	Key Ideas and Details	Central Idea	Text Organization
Forest Fire!	Informational Text/Interview	J	490L	Key Ideas and Details	Content-Area Words	Ideas and Support
Gibbons, The Singing Apes	Informational Text	J	500L	Key Ideas and Details	Central Idea	Author's Purpose
Homes for Everyone	Informational Text	J	490L	Key Ideas and Details	Central Idea	Content-Area Words
Ice	Procedural Text	J	420L	Key Ideas and Details	Author's Purpose	Text Organization
Many Ways to Work	Informational Text	J	520L	Key Ideas and Details	Content-Area Words	Central Idea
Ms. Higgs Starts School	Realistic Fiction	J	530L	Key Ideas and Details	Story Structure	Characters
Mystery of the Bay Monster	Mystery	J	540L	Key Ideas and Details	Point of View	Connect Text and Visuals
Our Day in the Big City	Realistic Fiction	J	510L	Key Ideas and Details	Characters	Setting
The Bags by the Gate	Realistic Fiction	J	490L	Key Ideas and Details	Setting	Story Structure
The Mystery of the Clever Cat	Mystery	J	500L	Key Ideas and Details	Author's Purpose	Story Structure
The Princess and the Peas	Fairy Tale	J	460L	Key Ideas and Details	Story Structure	Theme

Rigby Leveled Library

Grade 2 *continued*

Title	Genre	Guided Reading Level	Lexile	Take & Teach Instructional Sessions		
The Scooter Race	Realistic Fiction	J	540L	Key Ideas and Details	Point of View	Text and Graphic Features
A Friend for Ben	Realistic Fiction	K	520L	Key Ideas and Details	Story Structure	Setting
A Visit to Gold Town	Realistic Fiction	K	600L	Key Ideas and Details	Author's Purpose	Setting
Animal Helpers	Informational Text	K	500L	Key Ideas and Details	Text and Graphic Features	Central Idea
Ben Franklin	Biography	K	800L	Key Ideas and Details	Central Idea	Text and Graphic Features
Dairy Farmers	Informational Text	K	510L	Key Ideas and Details	Text Organization	Central Idea
Emily's Surprise	Realistic Fiction	K	520L	Key Ideas and Details	Story Structure	Characters
Frogs	Informational Text	K	540L	Key Ideas and Details	Central Idea	Text and Graphic Features
Heroes in the Sky	Biography	K	560L	Key Ideas and Details	Ideas and Support	Point of View
Lucky Socks	Realistic Fiction	K	500L	Key Ideas and Details	Characters	Theme
Plants Need Water	Procedural Text	K	450L	Key Ideas and Details	Text Organization	Author's Purpose
The Singing Princess	Fairy Tale	K	490L	Key Ideas and Details	Figurative Language	Connect Text and Visuals
The Wind and the Sun	Fable	K	540L	Key Ideas and Details	Figurative Language	Theme
Where Is Hoppy?	Realistic Fiction	K	570L	Key Ideas and Details	Connect Text and Visuals	Story Structure
Why Coyote Howls at the Moon	Folktale	K	570L	Key Ideas and Details	Characters	Story Structure
Winter	Informational Text	K	540L	Key Ideas and Details	Central Idea	Author's Purpose
All About Masks	Informational Text	L	540L	Key Ideas and Details	Author's Purpose	Ideas and Support
Black Rhinos	Informational Text	L	540L	Key Ideas and Details	Text Organization	Central Idea
Finding Talent	Realistic Fiction	L	560L	Key Ideas and Details	Story Structure	Figurative Language
Flightless Birds	Informational Text	L	490L	Key Ideas and Details	Central Idea	Text Organization
How to Put On a Class Play	Realistic Fiction	L	610L	Key Ideas and Details	Point of View	Content-Area Words
Large Trucks	Informational Text	L	600L	Key Ideas and Details	Text and Graphic Features	Central Idea
Lizards	Informational Text	L	530L	Key Ideas and Details	Central Idea	Content-Area Words
The Cicada Concert	Realistic Fiction	L	560L	Key Ideas and Details	Setting	Characters
The Guinea Pig Rescue	Realistic Fiction	L	480L	Key Ideas and Details	Connect Text and Visuals	Characters
The Storm	Realistic Fiction	L	520L	Key Ideas and Details	Story Structure	Theme
The Wonderful Water Cycle	Informational/Procedural Text	L	500L	Key Ideas and Details	Text Organization	Text and Graphic Features
What's Up? Watching the Night Sky	Informational Text	L	590L	Key Ideas and Details	Text Organization	Text and Graphic Features
Why the Leopard Has Spots	Folktale	L	500L	Key Ideas and Details	Setting	Author's Purpose

LITERATURE RESOURCES

Grade 2 continued

Title	Genre	Guided Reading Level	Lexile	Take & Teach Instructional Sessions		
Winter Sports	Informational Text	L	620L	Key Ideas and Details	Ideas and Support	Text and Graphic Features
Zac's New Act	Realistic Fiction	L	630L	Key Ideas and Details	Characters	Connect Text and Visuals
All About Sharks	Informational/Opinion Text	M	600L	Key Ideas and Details	Ideas and Support	Text and Graphic Features
An Encyclopedia of Fossils	Informational Text	M	590L	Key Ideas and Details	Author's Purpose	Text and Graphic Features
Bug-head and Me	Realistic Fiction	M	670L	Key Ideas and Details	Point of View	Story Structure
Camp Buddies	Realistic Fiction	M	520L	Key Ideas and Details	Characters	Theme
Exercise for Everyone	Informational/Procedural Text	M	590L	Key Ideas and Details	Text Organization	Author's Purpose
Jungle Jenny	Realistic Fiction	M	670L	Key Ideas and Details	Figurative Language	Characters
Kitchen Table Science	Procedural Text	M	480L	Key Ideas and Details	Text Organization	Text and Graphic Features
Olivia's First Surf	Realistic Fiction	M	610L	Key Ideas and Details	Setting	Theme
Space Vacation	Science Fiction/Fantasy	M	560L	Key Ideas and Details	Story Structure	Setting
The Japanese Giant Hornet	Informational Text	M	700L	Key Ideas and Details	Central Idea	Content-Area Words
The Moon Festival	Realistic Fiction	M	530L	Key Ideas and Details	Text and Graphic Features	Point of View
The Travelers and the Bear	Fable	M	740L	Key Ideas and Details	Characters	Author's Purpose
Tracker Dogs	Realistic Fiction/Informational Text	M	970L	Key Ideas and Details	Content-Area Words	Text Organization
Vr-oo-m!	Realistic Fiction	M	530L	Key Ideas and Details	Point of View	Story Structure
Whoosh! The Story of Snowboarding	Informational Text	M	600L	Key Ideas and Details	Central Idea	Ideas and Support
A Ship Is Coming!	Realistic Fiction	N	550L	Key Ideas and Details	Theme	Point of View
Bug on the Beam	Realistic Fiction/Diary	N	680L	Key Ideas and Details	Theme	Connect Text and Visuals
Did You Hear?	Realistic Fiction	N	600L	Key Ideas and Details	Story Structure	Theme
Flamenco Music and Dance	Informational Text	N	490L	Key Ideas and Details	Central Idea	Ideas and Support
I Wonder...	Informational Text	N	570L	Key Ideas and Details	Content-Area Words	Ideas and Support
Mount St. Helens: A Mountain Explodes	Informational Text/Journal	N	630L	Key Ideas and Details	Text Organization	Content-Area Words
My Frog Log	Informational Text	N	560L	Key Ideas and Details	Author's Purpose	Connect Text and Visuals
Our Changing Earth: An Encyclopedia of Landforms	Informational Text	N	850L	Key Ideas and Details	Text Organization	Author's Purpose
Rain Forest Encyclopedia	Informational Text	N	560L	Key Ideas and Details	Text and Graphic Features	Ideas and Support

Rigby Leveled Library

Grade 2 continued

Title	Genre	Guided Reading Level	Lexile	Take & Teach Instructional Sessions		
Saving the Hens	Realistic Fiction	N	580L	Key Ideas and Details	Story Structure	Point of View
Teeth	Informational Text	N	560L	Key Ideas and Details	Text and Graphic Features	Central Idea
The Mystery Mask	Mystery	N	800L	Key Ideas and Details	Figurative Language	Setting
Trouble on the Trail	Realistic Fiction	N	840L	Key Ideas and Details	Characters	Story Structure
What a Night!	Realistic Fiction	N	580L	Key Ideas and Details	Setting	Theme
Woodland People, Desert People	Informational Text	N	650L	Key Ideas and Details	Text and Graphic Features	Content-Area Words

Credits

Cover: *all photos* ©Carrie Garcia/HMH

Tablets used multiple times ©Mr Aesthetics/Shutterstock

Circular festive pattern used multiple times ©ksana-art/Shutterstock

All other photos: 2 *holding tablet* ©Veja/Shutterstock; 3 *shoes* ©Rose Carson/Shutterstock; 3 *teacher and students* ©wavebreakmedia/Shutterstock; 4 *Alma Flor Ada* ©F. Isabel Campoy; 4 *Kylene Beers* ©Heinemann Educational Publishing; 4 *F. Isabel Campoy* ©Josh Edelson/Houghton Mifflin Harcourt; 4 *Joyce Armstrong Carroll* ©Anthony Rathbun/Houghton Mifflin Harcourt; 4 *Nathan Clemens* ©George Brainard/Houghton Mifflin Harcourt; 4 *Anne Cunningham* ©Josh Edelson/Houghton Mifflin Harcourt; 4 *Martha C. Hougen* ©Danny Moloshok/Houghton Mifflin Harcourt; 4 *Dr. Tyrone C. Howard* ©Abigail Bobo/HMH; 4 *Elena Izquierdo* ©Andres Leighton/Houghton Mifflin Harcourt; 4 *Carol Jago* ©Andrew Collings Photography; 5 *Erik Palmer* ©Kellie Henricksen/Kellie Henriksen; 5 *Robert E. Probst* ©Heinemann Educational Publishing; 5 *Shane Templeton* ©Tom Smedes/Houghton Mifflin Harcourt; 5 *Julie Washington* ©John Amis/Houghton Mifflin Harcourt; 5 *David Dockterman* ©Scott Eisen/Houghton Mifflin Harcourt; 5 *Jill Eggleton* ©Jill Eggleton QSO; 7 *all students* ©Rawpixel.com/Shutterstock; 9 *student* ©Ogla Nikiforova/Shutterstock; 11 ©Helder Almeida/Shutterstock; 12 ©Veja/Shutterstock; 13 ©wavebreakmedia/Shutterstock; 14 *shoes* ©Rose Carson/Shutterstock; 15 *students and teacher* ©wavebreakmedia/Shutterstock; 16 ©wavebreakmedia/Shutterstock; 17 *all students* ©Rawpixel.com/Shutterstock; 18 *all teachers* ©Rawpixel.com/Shutterstock; 21 *teacher and students* ©wavebreakmedia/Shutterstock; 25 ©Brocreative/Shutterstock; 32 *hands* ©WAYHOME studio/Shutterstock; 32 *tablet* ©Alexey Boldin/Shutterstock; 33 *teacher and students* ©michaeljung/Shutterstock; 34 ©Carrie Garcia/HMH; 98 *filing box* ©Carrie Garcia/HMH; 99 *observation notes* ©Carrie Garcia/HMH; 114 ©Betsy Hansen/HMH; 115-117 *all photos* ©Carrie Garcia/HMH; 122 ©Betsy Hansen/HMH; 126 *Alma Flor Ada* ©F. Isabel Campoy; 126 *F. Isabel Campoy* ©Josh Edelson/HMH; 126 *Elena Izquierdo* ©Andres Leighton/HMH; 128 *athletes image on tablet* ©Scott Barbour/Getty Images; 134 ©Steve Williams/HMH